THE SEARCH WARRANT

PATRICK MODIANO was born in an outlying quarter of Paris in 1945. He published his first novel, *La Place de l'Étoile*, when he was 21, and has made a distinguished career as a novelist ever since. He has won the Grand Prix du Roman de l'Académie Française and the Prix Goncourt. His fiction is haunted by the trauma of the German Occupation of France, and this subject also features in the screenplay of *Lacombe Lucien* which he wrote for the film director Louis Malle.

JOANNA KILMARTIN is the translator and editor of Marcel Proust's *Selected Letters: Volume Four, 1918–1922*. She has been awarded the Scott-Moncrieff translation prize twice: in 1971 for *Sunlight on Cold Water* by Françoise Sagan, and in 1974 for *Bernadini's Terrace* by Suzanne Prou.

Also by Patrick Modiano in English translation

Patrick Modiano

THE SEARCH
WARRANT

Translated from the French by
Joanna Kilmartin

THE HARVILL PRESS
LONDON

First published with the title *Dora Bruder* by Éditions Gallimard, Paris, 1997

First published in Great Britain in 2000 by
The Harvill Press
2 Aztec Row
Berners Road
London N1 0PW

1 3 5 7 9 8 6 4 2

www.harvill.com

This publication is supported by the French Ministry for
Foreign Affairs, as part of the Burgess programme headed for the French
Embassy in London by the Institut Français du Royaume-Uni

Ï institut français

This edition has also been published with the
financial assistance of the French Ministry of Culture

Patrick Modiano asserts the moral right to be
identified as the author of this work

A CIP catalogue record for this book is
available from the British Library

ISBN 1 86046 612 5

Designed and typeset in Fournier at
Libanus Press, Marlborough, Wiltshire

Printed and bound in Great Britain by
Butler and Tanner Ltd at Selwood Printing, Burgess Hill

THE SEARCH WARRANT

Eight years ago, in an old copy of *Paris Soir* dated 31 December 1941, a heading on page three caught my eye: "From Day to Day".* Below this, I read:

PARIS

Missing, a young girl, Dora Bruder, age 15, height 1.55m, oval-shaped face, grey-brown eyes, grey sports jacket, maroon pullover, navy-blue skirt and hat, brown gym shoes. Address all information to M. and Mme Bruder, 41 Boulevard Ornano, Paris.

I had long been familiar with the area around the Boulevard Ornano. As a child, I would accompany my mother to the Saint-Ouen flea markets. We would get off the bus either at the Porte de Clignancourt or, occasionally, outside the 18th arrondissement Town Hall. Always, it

* "*D'hier à aujourd'hui*".

3

was a Saturday or Sunday afternoon.

In winter, on the tree-shaded pavement outside Clignancourt barracks, the fat photographer with the round spectacles and a lumpy nose who offered "souvenir snaps" would set up his tripod amid the stream of passers-by. In summer, he stationed himself on the broadwalk at Deauville, outside the Bar du Soleil. There, he found plenty of customers. But here, at the Porte de Clignancourt, people seemed not to wish to be photographed. His overcoat was shabby and he had a hole in one shoe.

I remember the Boulevard Ornano and the Boulevard Barbès one sunny afternoon in May 1958, deserted. A knot of riot police at each crossroads because of the Algerian situation.

I was in the neighbourhood in the winter of 1965. I had a girlfriend who lived in the Rue Championnet, Ornano 49–20.

Already, by that time, the Sunday stream of passers-by outside the barracks must have swept away the fat photographer, though I never went back to check. What were they used for, those barracks?* I was told they were occupied by colonial troops.

January 1965. Dusk comes at around six o'clock to

* During the Occupation of Paris, Clignancourt barracks housed French volunteers serving in the Waffen SS. See David Pryce-Jones, *Paris in the Third Reich*. London: Collins, 1981.

4

the crossroads of the Boulevard Ornano and the Rue Championnet. I was non-existent, I blended into that twilight, into those streets.

The last café at the top of Boulevard Ornano on the right was called the "Verse Toujours".* There was another, on the left, at the corner of the Boulevard Ney, with a jukebox. The Ornano-Championnet crossroads had a chemist and a couple of cafés, the one on the corner of the Rue Duhesme being the older of the two.

The time I've spent, waiting in those cafés ... First thing in the morning, when it was still dark. Early in the evening, at dusk. Later on, at closing time ...

That Sunday evening, an old black sports car – it looked to me like a Jaguar – was parked outside the nursery school on the Rue Championnet. It bore a sign on the rear: Disabled Ex-Serviceman. The presence of such a car in this neighbourhood surprised me. I tried to imagine what its owner might look like.

After nine o'clock, the boulevard was deserted. I could still see lights at the mouth of Simplon métro station and, almost opposite, in the foyer of the Cinéma Ornano 43. I had never really noticed the building next to the cinema, no. 41, even though I had been passing it for months, for years. From 1965 to 1968. Address all information to M. and Mme Bruder, 41 Boulevard Ornano, Paris.

* "Keep Pouring"

From day to day. With the passage of time, perspectives become blurred for me, one winter merging into another. That of 1965 and that of 1942.

In 1965, I knew nothing of Dora Bruder. But now, 30 years on, it seems to me that those long waits in the cafés at the Ornano crossroads, those unvarying itineraries – the Rue du Mont Cenis took me back to the Butte Montmartre hotels, the Roma or the Alsina or the Terrass, Rue Caulaincourt – and the fleeting impressions I have retained: snatches of conversation heard on a spring evening beneath the trees in the Square Clignancourt, and again, in winter, on the way down to Simplon and the Boulevard Ornano, all that was not simply due to chance. Perhaps, although as yet unaware of it, I was on the track of Dora Bruder and her parents. Already, imperceptibly, they were there.

I am trying to search for clues, going far, far back in time. When I was about twelve, on those visits to the Clignancourt flea markets with my mother, at the top on the right of one of those aisles bordered by stalls, the Marché Malik or the Marché Vernaison, there was a young Polish Jew who sold suitcases ... Luxury suitcases, in leather or crocodile-skin, cardboard suitcases, travelling bags, cabin trunks labelled with the names of transatlantic companies – all heaped one on top of the other. His was an open-air stall. He was never without a cigarette dangling from the corner of his lips and, one afternoon, he offered me one.

*

Occasionally, I would go to one of the cinemas on the Boulevard Ornano. To the Clignancourt Palace at the top of the boulevard, next to the "Verse Toujours". Or else to the Ornano 43.

I discovered later that the Ornano 43 was a very old cinema. It had been rebuilt in the 1930s when it was made to look like an ocean liner. I returned to the area in May 1996. A shop had replaced the cinema. Carry on across the Rue Hermel and you come to 41 Boulevard Ornano, the address given in the notice about the missing Dora Bruder.

A five-story block of flats, late nineteenth century. Together with no. 39, it forms a single building, enclosed

7

by the boulevard, the top of the Rue Hermel, and the Rue Simplon which runs along the back of both blocks. These are matching. A plaque on no. 39 gives the name of the architect, a certain Pierrefeu, and the date of construction: 1881. The same must be true of no. 41.

Before the war, and up to the beginning of the 1950s, no. 41 had been a hotel, as had no. 39, which was called the Hôtel Lion d'Or. No. 39 also had a café-restaurant before the war, owned by a man named Gazal. I haven't discovered the name of the hotel at no. 41. In the early 1950s, the Ornano Hotel & Studios Company was listed in the telephone directory under this address: Montmartre 12–54. As was, then and before the war, a café with a proprietor by the name of Marchal. This café no longer exists. Would it have been to the right or the left of the *porte-cochère*?

This opens on to a longish corridor. At the far end, a staircase leads off to the right.

It takes time for what has been erased to resurface. Traces survive in registers, and nobody knows where these registers are hidden, and who has custody of them, and whether or not their custodians are willing to let you see them. Or perhaps they have simply forgotten that such registers exist.

All it takes is a little patience.

Thus, I came to learn that Dora Bruder and her parents were already living in the hotel on the Boulevard Ornano in 1937 and 1938. They had a room with a kitchenette on the fifth floor, the level at which an iron balcony encircles both blocks. The level with ten or so windows. Two or three give on to the boulevard, the rest on to the Rue Hermel or, at the back, the Rue Simplon.

When I revisited the neighbourhood on that day in May 1996, I noticed that the rusting shutters to the two end fifth-floor windows overlooking the Rue Simplon were closed, and that on the balcony outside there was a collection of miscellaneous objects, seemingly long abandoned there.

Sometime during the last three or four years before the war, Dora Bruder would have been enrolled at one of the local State secondary schools. I wrote to ask if her name was to be found on the school registers, addressing my letter to the head of each:

8 Rue Ferdinand-Flocon

20 Rue Hermel

7 Rue Championnet

61 Rue de Clignancourt

All replied politely. None had found this name on the list of their pre-war pupils. In the end, the head of the former girls' school at 69 Rue Championnet suggested that I come and consult the register for myself. One of these days, I shall. But I'm in two minds. I want to go on hoping that her name is there. It was the school nearest to where she lived.

*

It took me four years to discover her exact date of birth: 25 February 1926. And a further two years to find out her place of birth: Paris, 12th arrondissement. But I am a patient man. I can wait for hours in the rain.

*

One Friday afternoon in February 1996 I went to the 12th arrondissement Register Office. The registrar – a young man – handed me a form:

To be completed by the person applying for the certificate. Fill in your:
Surname:
Forename:
Address:

I require a full copy of the Birth Certificate for:
Surname: BRUDER Forename: DORA
Date of birth: 25 February 1926
Tick if you are:
The person in question
The father or mother
The grandfather or grandmother
The son or daughter
The husband or wife
The legal representative
You have power of attorney, and an identity card for the person in question.
Nobody other than the above persons may be supplied with a copy of a Birth Certificate.

I signed the form and handed it back to him. After reading it through, he said that he was unable to supply me with a full copy of the birth certificate: I bore no legal relationship to the person in question.

At first, I took him for one of those sentinels of oblivion whose role is to guard a shameful secret and deny access to anybody seeking to uncover even so much as a trace of a person's existence. But he was a decent fellow. He advised me to go to the Palais de Justice, 2 Boulevard du Palais, and apply for a special exemption from the Superintendent Registrar, Section 3, 5th floor, Staircase 5, Room 501. Open Monday to Friday, 2 to 4 p.m.

I was about to enter the main courtyard through the big iron gates at 2 Boulevard du Palais when a functionary directed me to another entrance a little farther on: the same as that for the Sainte Chapelle. I wanted to go straight through the porch, past the queue of tourists waiting behind the barriers, but another functionary gestured at me impatiently to queue up with the rest.

At the back of the foyer, regulations required one to empty one's pockets of anything metal. I had nothing on me except a bunch of keys. This I was supposed to place on a sort of conveyor belt for collection on the far side of a glass partition, but for a moment I couldn't think what to do. My hesitation earned me a rebuke from another functionary. Was he a policeman? A detective? Was I also supposed to hand over my shoelaces, belt, wallet, as at the gates of a prison?

I crossed a courtyard, followed a corridor, and emerged on to a vast concourse milling with men and women carrying black briefcases, some dressed in barristers' robes. I dared not ask them how to get to Staircase 5.

A commissionaire seated at a table directed me to the back of the concourse. And there I made my way into a deserted hall where overhead windows let in a dim, grey light. I walked this hall from end to end without finding Staircase 5. I was seized with panic, and with that sense of vertigo you have in a bad dream when you can't get to the station, time is running out and you are about to miss your train.

Twenty years before, I had had a similar experience. I had learnt that my father was in hospital, in the Pitié-Salpêtrière. I hadn't seen him since the end of my adolescent years. I therefore decided to pay him an impromptu visit.

I remember wandering for hours through the vastness of that hospital in search of him. I found my way into ancient buildings, into communal wards lined with beds, I questioned nurses who gave me contradictory directions. I came to doubt my father's existence, passing and re-passing that majestic church, and those spectral buildings, unchanged since the seventeenth century, which, for me, evoke Manon Lescaut and the era when, under the sinister appellation "General Hospital", the place was used as a prison for prostitutes awaiting deportation to Louisiana. I tramped the cobblestoned courtyards till dusk. It was impossible to find my father. I never saw him again.

But I found Staircase 5 in the end. I climbed the five flights. A row of offices. Somebody directed me to the one marked 501. A bored-looking woman with cropped hair asked me what I wanted.

Curtly, she informed me that to obtain particulars of a birth certificate I would have to write to the Public Prosecutor,* Department B, 14 Quai des Orfèvres, Paris 3.

Three weeks later I received a reply.

> At 09.10h. twenty-fifth February nineteen hundred and twenty-six, at 15 Rue Santerre, a female child, Dora, was born to Ernest Bruder, unskilled labourer, born Vienna (Austria) twenty-first May eighteen hundred and ninety-nine, and to his wife, Cécile Burdej, housewife, born Budapest (Hungary) seventeenth April nineteen hundred and seven, both domiciled at 2 Avenue Liégeard, Sevran (Seine-et-Oise). Registered at 15.30h. twenty-seventh February nineteen hundred and twenty-six on the affirmation of Gaspard Meyer, aged seventy-three, employed and domiciled at 76 Rue de Picpus, he having been present at the birth and having read and signed it with Us, Auguste Guillaume Rossi, Deputy Mayor, 12th arrondissement, Paris.

* An official who has a number of non-judicial functions in France.

14

15 Rue Santerre is the address of the Rothschild Hospital. Many children of poor Jewish families, recent immigrants to France, were born in its maternity ward around the same time as Dora. Seemingly, on that Thursday of 25 February 1926, Ernest Bruder had been unable to get time off from work in order to register his daughter himself at the 12th arrondissement Town Hall. Perhaps there is a register somewhere which would provide more information about the Gaspard Meyer who had signed the birth certificate. 76 Rue de Picpus, where he was "employed and domiciled", was the address of the Rothschild Hospice, an establishment for the old and indigent.

In that winter of 1926, all trace of Dora Bruder and her parents peters out in Sevran, the suburb bordering the Ourcq canal to the north-east. One day I shall go to Sevran, but I fear that, as in all suburbs, houses and streets will have changed beyond recognition. Here are the names of a few businesses and inhabitants of the Avenue Liégeard dating from that period: no. 24 was the Freinville Trianon. Was this a café? A cinema? The Île-de-France Wine Cellars occupied no. 31. There was a Dr Jorand at no. 9, a chemist, Platel, at no. 30.

The Avenue Liégeard where Dora's parents lived was part of a built-up area which sprawled across the boroughs of Sevran, Livry-Gargan and Aulnay-sous-Bois and was known as Freinville.[*] It had grown up around the Westinghouse Brake Factory, established there at the beginning of the century. A working-class area. In the 1930s, it had tried to gain its automony, without success, and so had remained a dependency of the three adjoining boroughs. But it had its own railway station nevertheless: Freinville.

In that winter of 1926, Ernest Bruder, Dora's father, is sure to have been employed at the Westinghouse Brake Factory.

[*] The equivalent of Brakesville, from *frein*, a brake.

Ernest Bruder, born Vienna, Austria, 21 May 1899. His childhood would have been spent in that city's Jewish quarter, Leopoldstadt. His own parents were almost certainly natives of Galicia or Bohemia or Moravia, having come, like the majority of Vienna's Jews, from the eastern provinces of the Empire.

I had turned 20 in Vienna, in 1965, also the year when I was frequenting the Clignancourt districts. I lodged on the Taubstummengasse, behind Karlskirche. My first few nights were spent in a seedy hotel near the Western Station. I have memories of summer evenings spent in Sievering and Grinzing, and of parks where bands were playing. And, not far from Heilingenstadt, of a shack in the middle of some sort of allotment. Everything was closed on those July weekends, even the Café Hawelka. The city was deserted. Tramlines glittered in the sunlight, criss-crossing the north-western districts as far as Pötzleinsdorf Park.

Some day, I shall go back to Vienna, a city I haven't seen for over thirty years. Perhaps I shall find Ernest Bruder's birth certificate in the Register Office of Vienna's Jewish community. I shall learn his father's forename, occupation and birthplace, his mother's forename and maiden name. And whereabouts they had lived in that zone of the 2nd District, between the Northern Station, the Prater and the Danube.

Child and adolescent, he would have known the Prater, with its cafés, and its theatre, the home of the Budapester. And the Sweden Bridge. And the courtyard of the Commodities Exchange near the Taborstrasse. And the market square of the Carmelites.

In 1919, his life as a twenty-year-old in Vienna had been harder than mine. Following the first defeats of the Austrian army, tens of thousands of refugees fleeing from Galicia, Bukovina and the Ukraine had arrived in successive waves to crowd into the slums around the Northern Station. A city adrift, cut off from an Empire which had ceased to exist. Ernest Bruder must have been indistinguishable from the bands of unemployed roaming the streets of shuttered shops.

Or did he come from a less poverty-stricken background than the refugees from the east? The son of a Taborstrasse shopkeeper, perhaps? How can one know?

On a file-card, one of thousands in an index created some twenty years later to facilitate the round-up of Jews during the Occupation, and which still lies around to this day in the War Veterans Ministry, Ernest Bruder is described as "French legionnaire, 2nd class". So he must have enlisted in the Foreign Legion, though I have no means of knowing precisely when. 1919? 1920?

A man signed on for five years. He didn't even need to go to France, it was enough to visit a French Consulate. Was that what Ernest Bruder did, in Austria? Or was he already in France by then? Either way, along with other Germans and Austrians in his situation, he was probably posted to the barracks at Belfort or Nancy, where you were not exactly handled with kid gloves. Then it was Marseille and the Fort Saint-Nicolas, where the welcome was cooler still. After that, the troopship: apparently in Morocco, Lyautey was short of 30,000 men.

I'm trying to reconstitute Ernest Bruder's tour of duty. The bounty, handed out at Sidi Bel Abbès. The majority of enlisted men – Germans, Austrians, Russians, Romanians, Bulgarians – are so miserably poor that they are dazed by the idea of receiving this bounty. They can't believe their luck. Hastily, they stuff the cash into their pockets, as if they might be asked to give it back. Then comes the training, the long runs over the dunes, the interminable marches under a leaden African sun. For volunteers from central Europe, like Ernest Bruder, it is hard going: they have been undernourished throughout their adolescence, thanks to four years of war-time rationing.

Next, the barracks at Meknès, Fez or Marrakesh. They are sent on operations intended to pacify the still unsubjugated territories of Morocco.

April 1920. Skirmish at Bekrit and the Ras-Tarcha. June 1921. Skirmish on the Hayane Djebel under Colonel Lambert's battalion. March 1922. Skirmish of the Chouf-ech-Cherg. Captain Roth. May 1922. Skirmish at Tizi Adni. Nicolas's battalion. April 1923. Skirmishes at Arbala and in the Taza corridor. May 1923. Fierce fighting for the Talrant Bab-Brida, taken under intense fire by Naegelin's legionnaires. On the night of the 26th, in a surprise attack, Naegelin's battalion occupies the Ichendirt massif. June 1923. Skirmish at Tadout. Naegelin's battalion takes the ridge. Legionnaires raise the tricolour over an important casbah to the sound of bugles. Skirmish at Oued Athia, where Barrière's battalion has to make two bayonet charges. Buchsenschutz's battalion takes entrenched positions on the ridge south of the Bou-Khamouj. Battle for the El-Mers Basin. July 1923. Fighting on the Immouzer plateau. Cattin's battalion. Buchsenschutz's battalion. Susini's and Jenoudet's battalions. August 1923. Skirmish at Oued Tamghilt.

At night, in this landscape of stone-strewn sand, did he dream of Vienna, the city of his birth, and the chestnut trees of the Hauptallee? The file of Ernest Bruder, "French legionnaire, 2nd class" also states: "100% disabled". In which of these battles was he wounded?

*

At the age of twenty-five, he was on the streets of Paris. The Legion must have released him from his engagement because of his war wound. I don't suppose he mentioned it to anybody. Not that anybody would have been interested. I'm virtually certain that he didn't receive a disability pension. He was never given French citizenship. In fact, I've seen his disability mentioned only once, and that was in one of the police files designed to facilitate the round-ups during the Occupation.

In 1924, Ernest Bruder married a young woman of 17, Cécile Burdej, born 17 April 1907 in Budapest. I don't know where this marriage took place, nor do I know the names of their witnesses. How did they happen to meet? Cécile Burdej had arrived in Paris the year before, with her parents, her brother and her four sisters. A Jewish family of Russian origin, they had probably settled in Budapest at the beginning of the century.

Life being as hard in Budapest as it was in Vienna after the First World War, they were forced to flee west yet again. They ended up in Paris, at the Jewish refuge in the Rue Lamarck. Within a month of their arrival, three of the girls, aged fourteen, twelve and ten, were dead of typhoid fever.

Were Cécile and Ernest Bruder already living in the Avenue Liégeard, Sevran, at the time of their marriage?

Or in a hotel in Paris? For the first years of their marriage, after Dora's birth, they always lived in hotel rooms.

*

They are the sort of people who leave few traces. Virtually anonymous. Inseparable from those Paris streets, those suburban landscapes where, by chance, I discovered they had lived. Often, what I know about them amounts to no more than a simple address. And such topographical precision contrasts with what we shall never know about their life – this blank, this mute block of the unknown.

I track down Ernest and Cécile Bruder's niece. I talk to her on the telephone. The memories which she retains of them are those of childhood, at once fuzzy and sharp. She remembers her uncle's gentleness, his kindness. The few details which I have noted down about their family come from her. She has heard it said that before they lived in the hotel on the Boulevard Ornano, Ernest, Cécile and their daughter Dora had lived in another hotel. In a street off the Rue des Poissonniers. I looked at the street map, and read her out a succession of names. Yes, that was it, the Rue Polonceau. But she has never heard any mention of Sevran, nor of Freinville, nor of the Westinghouse factory.

*

It is said that premises retain some stamp, however faint, of their previous inhabitants. Stamp: an imprint, hollow or in relief. Hollow, I should say, in the case of Ernest and Cécile Bruder, of Dora. I have a sense of absence, of emptiness, whenever I find myself in a place where they have lived.

Two hotels, for that date, in the Rue Polonceau: the name of the tenant, at no. 49, is given as Roquette. In the telephone directory he is listed under "Hôtel Vin". The owner of the other, at no. 32, as Charles Campazzi. As hotels, they had a bad reputation. Today, they no longer exist.

Often, around 1968, I would follow the boulevards as far as the arches of the overhead métro. My starting point was the Place Blanche. In December, a travelling fair occupied the open ground. Its lights grew dimmer the nearer you got to the Boulevard de la Chapelle. At the time, I knew nothing of Dora Bruder and her parents. I remember having a strange feeling as I followed the wall of Lariboisière Hospital, and again on crossing the railway tracks, as though I had penetrated the darkest part of Paris. But it was merely the contrast between the dazzling lights of the Boulevard de Clichy and the black, interminable wall, the penumbra beneath the métro arches ...

Nowadays, on account of the railway lines, the proximity of the Gare du Nord and the rattle of the high-speed trains overhead, I still think of this part of the Boulevard de la Chapelle as a network of escape routes . . . A place where nobody would stay for long. A crossroads from which each went his or her separate way to the four points of the compass.

All the same, I made a note of local schools where, if they still exist, I might find Dora Bruder's name in the register:

Nursery school: 3 Rue Saint-Luc.

Primary schools for girls: 11 Rue Cavé, 43 Rue des Poissonniers, Impasse d'Oran.

And, at the Porte de Clignancourt, the years slipped by till the outbreak of war. I know nothing about the Bruders during this time. Was Cécile already working as a "furrier's seamstress", or rather, as it says in the files, "salaried garment-worker"? Her niece thinks she was employed in a workshop near the Rue de Ruisseau, but she can't be sure. Was Ernest Bruder still working as an unskilled labourer, if not at the Westinghouse factory in Freinville, then elsewhere, in some other suburb? Or had he too found work in a garment workshop in Paris? In the file which they had drawn up on him during the Occupation, the one in which I had read "French legionnaire, 2nd class, 100% disabled", beside the words "trade or profession" it says: "None".

A few photographs from this period. The earliest, their wedding day. They are seated, their elbows resting on a sort of pedestal. She is enveloped in a long white veil that trails to the floor and seems to be knotted at her left ear. He wears a suit with a white bow tie. A photograph with their daughter, Dora. They are seated, Dora standing between them: she can't be more than two years old. A photograph of Dora, surely taken after a school prize-giving. She is aged twelve or thereabouts, and wears a white dress and ankle socks. She holds a book in her right hand. Her hair is crowned by a circlet of what appear to be white flowers. Her left hand rests on the edge of an enormous white cube patterned with rows of black geometric motifs, evidently a studio prop. Another photograph, taken in the same place at the same period, perhaps on the same day: the floor tiles are recognizable, as is the big white cube with black geometric motifs on which Cécile Bruder is perched. Dora stands on her left, in a high-necked dress, her left arm bent across her body so as to place her hand on her mother's shoulder. In another photograph with her mother, Dora is about twelve years old, her hair shorter than in the previous picture. They are standing in front of what appears to be an old wall, though it must be one of the photo-grapher's screens. Both wear black dresses with a white collar. Dora stands slightly in front and to the right of her mother. An oval-shaped photograph in which Dora is slightly older – thirteen or fourteen, with longer hair – and all three are in single file, their faces turned towards the camera: Dora and her mother, both in white blouses, and behind them, Ernest Bruder, in jacket and tie. A photograph of Cécile Bruder in front of what appears to be a suburban house. The left-hand wall in the foreground is a mass of ivy. She is sitting on a low balustrade beside three cement steps. She wears a light summer frock. In the background, the silhouette of a child with her back to the camera, her arms and legs bare, wearing either a black jumper or a bathing suit. Dora? And behind a wooden fence, the façade of another house, with a porch and a single upstairs window. Where could this be?

An earlier photograph of Dora alone, aged nine or ten. Caught in a ray of sunshine, entirely surrounded by shadow, she might be on a rooftop. Dressed in white blouse and socks, she stands, hand on hip, her right foot resting on the cement rim of what appears to be a large cage or aviary, although, owing to the shadow, one can't make out the animals or birds confined there. These shadows and patches of sunlight are those of a summer's day.

Other summer days were spent in Clignancourt. Her parents would take Dora to the Cinéma Ornano 43. It was just across the street. Or did she go on her own? From a very young age, according to her cousin, she had been rebellious, independent, keen on boys. The hotel room was far too cramped for three people.

As a child, she would have played in the Square Clignancourt. At times, this part of town seemed like a village. In the evenings, the neighbours would carry their chairs outside and sit on the pavement for a chat. Or take a lemonade together on the café terrace. Sometimes men who could have been either real goatherds or else peddlars from the fairs would come by with a few goats and sell you tall glasses of milk for almost nothing. The froth gave you a white moustache.

At the Porte de Clignancourt, a toll-gate and customs

barrier.* To its left, between the flea market and the tall apartment blocks of the Boulevard Ney, an entire district of shacks, warehouses, acacias and low-built houses, since pulled down. This wasteland had impressed me, aged fourteen. I thought I recognized it in two or three photographs, taken in winter: a kind of esplanade, a passing bus in view. A lorry at a standstill, as if for ever. Waiting beside an expanse of snow, a gipsy caravan and a black horse. And in the far background, the hazy outline of high buildings.

I remember experiencing for the first time that sense of emptiness which comes with the knowledge of what has been destroyed, razed to the ground. As yet, I was ignorant of the existence of Dora Bruder. Perhaps — in fact, I'm sure of it — she would wander the streets of this zone which, for me, evokes secret lovers' trysts, pitiful moments of lost happiness. Here, reminders of the countryside still surfaced in the street-names: Allée du Puits, Allée du Métro, Allée des Peupliers, Impasse des Chiens.

* One of the eighteenth century gates (*barrières*) in the fortifications of Paris; originally control points for game; later also used to control goods bearing excise duty, they were abolished in the late 1920s.

On 9 May 1940, at the age of fourteen, Dora Bruder was enrolled in the boarding school of the Convent of The Holy Heart of Mary, run by the Sisters of the Christian Schools of Divine Mercy[*] at 60–62 Rue de Picpus in the 12th arrondissement.

The school register contains the following entry:

Name and forename: Bruder, Dora.

Date and place of birth: 25 February 1926, Paris 12, to Ernest and Cécile Bruder *née* Brudej.

Family status: legitimate.

Date and conditions of admission: 9 May 1940. Full boarder.

Date and reason for departure: 14 December 1941. Pupil has run away.

[*] The Écoles Chrétiennes de la Miséricorde ran the boarding school Saint-Coeur-de-Marie.

What were her parents' reasons for sending her to this religious school? No doubt it was difficult living three to a room in the Boulevard Ornano hotel. I wonder if Ernest and Cécile Bruder, as ex-Austrians and "citizens of the Reich", were not threatened with a form of internment, Austria having ceased to exist in 1938 and become part of the "Reich".

In the autumn of 1939, men who were ex-Austrian or otherwise citizens of the "Reich" were interned in "assembly camps". They were divided into two categories: suspect and non-suspect. Non-suspects were taken to the Yves-du-Manoir stadium at Colombe. Then, in December, they were included with the group known as "foreign statute labourers". Was Ernest Bruder among those labourers?

On 13 May 1940, four days after Dora Bruder's arrival at the Convent of The Holy Heart of Mary, ex-Austrian women and citizens of the Reich were called up in their turn and taken to the Vélodrome d'Hiver, where they were interned for thirteen days. Then, with the approach of the German army, they were transferred to the camp at Gurs, in the Basses-Pyrénées. Was Cécile Bruder among those called-up?

You were placed in bizarre categories you had never heard of and which bore no relation to who you really were. You were called up. You were interned. If only you could understand why.

*

I also wonder how Cécile and Ernest Bruder came to hear of the Convent of The Holy Heart of Mary. Who had advised them to send Dora there?

I imagine that, by the age of fourteen, she must have given proof of independence, and that the rebellious spirit which her cousin had mentioned to me would already have manifested itself. Her parents felt that she was in need of discipline. For this, these Jews chose a Christian institution. But were they themselves practising Jews? And what choice did they have? According to the biographical note on the institution's Mother Superior at the time when Dora was a boarder there, the pupils at the Convent of The Holy Heart of Mary came from poor backgrounds: "Often, they are orphans, or children dependent on social welfare, those to whom Our Lord has always given His special love." And, in a brochure on the Sisters of the Christian Schools of Divine Mercy: "The vocation of the Holy Heart of Mary is to render signal service to infants and young girls from the capital's underprivileged families."

The teaching certainly went beyond the arts of sewing and housekeeping. The Sisters of the Christian Schools of Divine Mercy, whose mother house was the ancient abbey of Saint-Sauveur-le-Vicomte in Normandy, had founded the charitable institution of The Holy Heart of Mary, Rue de Picpus, in 1852. In those days, it was a vocational boarding school for 500 girls, the daughters of working men's families, with a staff of seventy-five nuns.

※

At the time of the fall of France in June 1940, nuns and pupils were evacuated to the department of Maine-et-Loire. Dora would have left with them, on one of the last packed trains still running from the Gare d'Orsay and the Gare d'Austerlitz. They were following in the footsteps of the long cortège of refugees on the routes leading south to the Loire.

July, and the return to Paris. Boarding school life. I don't know what the school uniform consisted of. Was it, quite simply, the clothes listed in the notice about the search for Dora: maroon pullover, navy-blue skirt, brown gym shoes? And, over this, a smock? I can more or less guess the daily timetable. Rise about six. Chapel. Classroom. Refectory. Classroom. Playground. Refectory. Classroom. Chapel. Dormitory. Day of rest, Sunday. I imagine that life behind those walls was hard for these girls for whom Our Lord has always shown His special love.

I have heard that the Sisters of the Christian Schools of Divine Mercy of the Rue de Picpus had established a holiday camp at Béthisy. Was this Béthisy-Saint-Martin?

Or Béthisy-Saint-Pierre? Both villages are near Senlis, in the Valois. Perhaps Dora Bruder and her classmates spent a few days there, in the summer of 1941.

*

The buildings of the Holy Heart of Mary no longer exist. Modern apartment blocks have taken their place, giving an idea of the vastness of the grounds. I don't possess a single photograph of the vanished school. On an old map of Paris, its site is marked "House of religious education". Four little squares and a cross symbolize the convent buildings and chapel. And a long, narrow rectangle, extending from the Rue de Picpus to the Rue de la Gare-de-Reuilly, outlines the perimeter of the grounds.

Opposite the convent, on the other side of the Rue de Picpus, the map shows, successively, the houses of The Community of the Mother of God, The Ladies of the Adoration and the Picpus Oratory and cemetery where, in the last months of the Terror, over one thousand victims of the guillotine were buried in a common grave. And on the same side of the street as the convent, almost an extension of it, the large property belonging to the Ladies of Sainte Clothilde. Then that of the Lady Deaconesses, where, one day, aged eighteen, I went for treatment. I remember their garden. I didn't know at the time that this establishment served as a rehabilitation centre for delinquent girls. Not unlike the Holy Heart of Mary. Not unlike The Good Shepherd. These institutions, where you were shut up, not knowing when or if you would be released, certainly rejoiced in some curious names: The Good Shepherd of Angers. The Refuge of Darnétal. The Sanctuary of Sainte Marie of Limoges. The Solitude of Nazareth.

Solitude.

*

The Holy Heart of Mary, 60–62 Rue de Picpus, stood at the corner of the Rue de Picpus and the Rue de la Gare-de-Reuilly. In Dora's time, this street still had a countrified air. A high wall ran the length of its left-hand side, shaded by the convent trees.

The few details which I have managed to glean about these places, such as Dora Bruder would have seen them, day in, day out, for a year and a half, are as follows: the large garden ran the length of the Rue de la Gare-de-Reuilly, and the convent buildings must have stood between it and the courtyard. Within this courtyard, hollowed out beneath rocks in the form of an imitation grotto, lay the burial vault of the Mardre family, the convent's benefactors.

I don't know if Dora Bruder made friends at the Holy Heart of Mary. Or if she kept to herself. Until such time as I have the testimony of one of her former classmates, I am reduced to conjecture. Today, in Paris, or somewhere in the suburbs, there must be a seventy-year-old woman who remembers her erstwhile neighbour in classroom or dormitory – a girl named Dora, age 15, height 1.55m, oval-shaped face, grey-brown eyes, grey sports jacket, maroon pullover, navy-blue skirt and hat, brown gym shoes.

In writing this book, I am sending out signals, like a lighthouse beacon in whose power to illuminate the darkness I have, alas, no faith. But I live in hope.

In those days, the Mother Superior of The Holy Heart of Mary was Marie-Jean-Baptiste. She was born – so her biographical note tells us – in 1903. After her novitiate, she was sent to Paris, to the house of The Holy Heart of Mary, where she stayed for seventeen years, from 1929 to 1946. She was barely forty years old when Dora Bruder was a boarder there.

She was "independent and warm-hearted" – according to the biographical note – and "endowed with a strong personality". She died in 1985, three years before I knew of Dora Bruder's existence. She would certainly have remembered Dora – if only because the girl had run away. But, after all, what could she have told me? A few details, the humdrum facts of daily existence? Warm-hearted or not, she certainly failed to divine what was going through Dora Bruder's head, neither how the girl was coping with boarding school life, nor what she thought of chapel morning and evening, the fake grotto in the courtyard, the garden wall, the dormitory with its rows of beds.

*

I traced a woman who had entered the convent in 1942, a few months after Dora Bruder ran away. She was about ten years old at the time, younger than Dora. And her memories of the Holy Heart of Mary are merely those of a child. She had been living alone with her mother, a Jew of Polish origin, in a street in the Goutte-d'Or district, the Rue de Chartres, no distance from the Rue Polonceau where Cécile, Ernest and Dora Bruder lived. To avoid dying of starvation, the mother worked night-shifts in a workshop that made mittens for the Wehrmacht. The daughter went to school in the Rue Jean-François Lépine. At the end of 1942, because of the round-ups, the headmistress advised her mother to send the child into hiding, and it was doubtless she who had given her the address of the Holy Heart of Mary.

To disguise her origins, she was enrolled at the convent under the name of "Suzanne Albert". Shortly afterwards, she fell ill. She was sent to the sanatorium. There, she was visited by a doctor. After a while, since she refused to eat, they decided they no longer wanted to keep her.

She remembers everything in that convent as being black – walls, classrooms, sanatorium – except for the white coifs of the nuns. It seemed more like an orphan-age. Iron discipline. No heating. Nothing to eat but root vegetables. Boarders' Prayers took place at six o'clock. I forgot to ask her whether she meant six o'clock in the morning or six o'clock at night.

Dora spent the summer of 1940 at the convent. On Sundays, she would certainly have gone to visit her parents, who were still living in the hotel room at 41 Boulevard Ornano. I look at the plan of the métro and try to retrace her route in my mind. The simplest, avoiding too many changes, is to take a train from Nation, a station fairly near the convent. Pont-de-Sèvres line. Change at Strasbourg-Saint-Denis. Porte de Clignancourt line. She would have got out at Simplon, just opposite the cinema and the hotel.

Twenty years later, I often took the métro from Simplon. It was always about ten o'clock at night. At that hour, the station was deserted, and there were long intervals between trains.

Late on Sunday afternoons, she too would have returned by the same route. Did her parents go with her? Once at Nation, she had to walk, and the quickest way to the Rue de Picpus was via the Rue Fabre-d'Églantine.

It was like going back to prison. The days were drawing in. It was already dark when she crossed the courtyard, passing the mausoleum with its imitation grotto. Above the steps, a single lamp was lit over the door. She followed the corridors. Chapel, for Sunday evening Prayers. Then, into line, in silence as far as the dormitory.

It is autumn. On 2 October, the Paris newspapers publish a decree obliging all Jews to register at police stations for a census. A declaration by the head of the family suffices for all. To avoid long queues, those concerned are asked to attend in alphabetical order, on the dates indicated in the table below . . .

The letter B fell on 4 October. On that day, Ernest Bruder went to Clignancourt police station to fill in the census form. But he failed to register his daughter. Everybody reporting for the census was allotted a number, which would later be attached to one's "family file". This was known as the "Jewish dossier" number.

Ernest and Cécile Bruder had the Jewish dossier number 49091. But Dora had no number of any sort.

Perhaps Ernest Bruder felt that she was out of harm's way, in a free zone, at the Convent of The Holy Heart of Mary, and that it was best not to draw attention to her. Then again, the classification "Jew" meant nothing to the fourteen-year-old Dora. When it came down to it, what did people understand by the term "Jew"? For himself, he never gave it a thought. He was used to being put into this or that category by the authorities, accepting it without question. Unskilled labourer. Ex-Austrian. French legionnaire. Non-suspect. Ex-serviceman 100% disabled. Foreign statute labourer. Jew. And the same went for his wife, Cécile. Ex-Austrian. Non-suspect. Furrier's seamstress. Jewess. As yet, the only person who had escaped all classification, including the number 49091, was Dora.

Who knows, she might have escaped to the end. She had only to remain within the dark walls of the convent, merging into their shadows; and to avoid drawing attention to herself by scrupulously observing the daily and nightly routine. Dormitory. Chapel. Refectory. Playground. Classroom. Chapel. Dormitory.

*

It chanced – but was it really chance? – that at the Convent of the Holy Heart of Mary she was back within sight of her birthplace across the street. 15 Rue Santerre. The Rothschild Hospital maternity ward. Rue Santerre was a continuation of the Rue de la Gare-de-Reuilly, and thus ran alongside the convent wall.

43

A quiet, tree-shaded neighbourhood. When, twenty-five years ago, in June 1971, I spent an entire day walking around there, I found it unchanged. Now and then, a summer shower would oblige me to shelter under a porch. That afternoon, without knowing why, I had the impression of walking in another's footsteps.

By the summer of '42, the area around the Holy Heart of Mary had become particularly dangerous. For two years there had been a succession of police swoops, on the Rothschild Hospital, on its orphanage, Rue Lamblardie, and on the Hospice, 76 Rue de Picpus, where the Gaspard Meyer who had signed Dora's birth certificate lived and worked. The Rothschild hospital, as far as the sick from the camp at Drancy were concerned, was a trap; they were sent there only to be returned to the camp whenever it suited the Germans, who kept a watch on 15 Rue Santerre with the help of a private detective agency, the Faralicq. A great many children and adolescents of Dora's age in hiding at the Rothschild orphanage, Rue Lamblardie, the first street on the right after the Rue de la Gare-de-Reuilly, were arrested there. And on the Rue de la Gare-de-Reuilly itself, at no. 48*bis*, exactly opposite the convent wall, nine boys and girls of Dora's age or, in some cases, younger, were arrested with their families. Indeed, the garden and courtyard of the Convent of The Holy Heart of Mary was the sole enclave in this entire block of houses to remain inviolate. But only on condition that you never

44

went out, that you stayed forgotten within the shadow
of those dark walls, which were in turn engulfed by the
darkness of the curfew.

*

I am writing these pages in November 1996. It seldom
stops raining. Tomorrow we shall be in December, and
fifty-five years will have passed since Dora ran away. It
gets dark early, and it is just as well: night obliterates
the greyness and monotony of these rainy days when
one wonders if it really is daytime, or if we are not going
through some intermediary stage, a sort of gloomy eclipse
lasting till dusk. Then the street-lamps and shop windows
and cafés light up, the evening air freshens, contours
sharpen, there are traffic jams at the crossroads and
hurrying crowds in the streets. And in the midst of all
these lights, all this hubbub, I can hardly believe that this
is the city where Dora lived with her parents, where my
father lived when he was twenty years younger than I
am now. I feel as if I am alone in making the link between
Paris then and Paris now, alone in remembering all these
details. There are moments when the link is stretched
to breaking-point, and other evenings when the city of
yesterday appears to me in fugitive gleams behind that
of today.

I have been re-reading the fifth and sixth volumes of
Les Misérables. Victor Hugo describes Cosette and Jean

Valjean, tracked by Javert, crossing Paris by night from the Saint-Jacques tollgate to the Petit Picpus. One can follow part of their itinerary on a map. As they near the Seine, Cosette begins to tire. Jean Valjean carries her in his arms. Taking the back streets, they skirt the Jardin des Plantes and come to the river bank. They cross the Pont d'Austerlitz. Scarcely has Jean Valjean set foot on the right bank than he thinks he sees shadowy figures on the bridge. The only hope of escape – he tells himself – is to take the little Rue du Chemin-Vert-Saint-Antoine.

And suddenly, one has a feeling of vertigo, as if Cosette and Jean Valjean, to escape Javert and his police, have taken a leap into space: thus far, they have been following real Paris streets, and now, abruptly, Victor Hugo thrusts them into the imaginary district of Paris which he calls the Petit Picpus. This feeling of not belonging is the same sensation which grips you in a dream, when you find yourself walking through an unfamiliar district. On waking, you realize, little by little, that the pattern of its streets had overlaid the one with which, in daytime, you are familiar.

And here is what disturbs me: at the end of their flight across a district whose topography and street-names have been invented by Victor Hugo, Cosette and Jean Valjean just manage to escape a police patrol by slipping behind a wall. They find themselves in "a garden, truly vast and of singular appearance: one of those gloomy gardens which seem made to be seen at night in winter".

This garden where the pair hide is that of a convent, which Victor Hugo situates precisely at no. 62 Rue de Petit-Picpus, the same address as that of the Convent of The Holy Heart of Mary where Dora was a boarder.

"At the time of this story", Victor Hugo writes, "a boarding school was attached to the convent. [...] The girls [...] were dressed in blue, with white caps. Three quite distinct buildings lay within this enclave of Petit Picpus, the main convent where the nuns lived, the boarding school for girls and, lastly, the house known as 'the little convent'."

And having given a minute description of the place, he continues: "We could not pass by this extraordinary, unknown, obscure building without entering it, nor without ushering in the minds of those who accompany us, and who listen as we relate, to the benefit of a few perhaps, the melancholy story of Jean Valjean."

*

Like many writers before me, I believe in coincidence and, sometimes, in the novelist's gift for clairvoyance – the word "gift" not being the right one, for it implies a kind of superiority. Clairvoyance is simply part of the profession: the essential leaps of imagination, the need to fix one's mind on detail – to the point of obsession, in fact – so as not to lose the thread and give in to one's natural laziness. All this tension, this cerebral exercise, may well lead in the long run to "flashes of intuition concerning events past and future", as defined by Larousse dictionary under "clairvoyance".

In December 1988, after reading the anouncement of the search for Dora in the *Paris Soir* of December 1941, I had thought about it incessantly for months. The precision of certain details haunted me: "41 Boulevard Ornano, 1.55m, oval-shaped face, grey-brown eyes, grey sports jacket, maroon pullover, navy-blue skirt and hat, brown gym shoes." And all enveloped in night, ignorance, forgetfulness, oblivion. It seemed impossible to me that I should ever find the faintest trace of Dora Bruder. At the time, the emptiness I felt prompted me to write a novel, *Honeymoon*,* it being as good a way as any of continuing to fix my attention on Dora Bruder, and perhaps, I told myself, of elucidating or divining something about her, a place where she had been, a detail of her life. I knew nothing about her parents, about the circumstances of her flight. All I had to go on was this: I had seen her name, BRUDER, DORA – nothing else, no date or place of birth – above that of her father – BRUDER, ERNEST, 21.5.99, Vienna. Stateless. – on the list of those who left on the convoy of 18 September 1942 for Auschwitz.

In writing *Honeymoon*, I had had in mind certain women I knew in the 1960s: Anne B., Bella D. – the same age as

* First published with the title *Voyage de Noces* by Éditions Gallimard, Paris, 1990 and published in Great Britain by Harvill, London, 1992.

Dora, in one case almost to the month – who could have shared her fate, having been in a similar situation during the Occupation, and whom she may have resembled. Today, it occurs to me that I had had to write 200 pages before I captured, unconsciously, a vague gleam of the truth.

It was a matter of a few lines: "The train stopped at Nation. The line didn't go any farther. Rigaud and Ingris had gone past Bastille, where they ought to have changed for the Porte Dorée. They came out of the métro into a big snowfield. [. . .] The sledge cut through several little streets to get to the Boulevard Soult." *

These back streets lay behind the Rue de Picus and the Holy Heart of Mary, the convent from which Dora Bruder made her escape, one December evening when it had probably been snowing in Paris.

That was the only moment in the book when, without knowing it, I came close to her in time and space.

* *Honeymoon*. Harvill, London, 1992.

Thus we find next to Dora Bruder's name in the school register, under the heading *Date and reason for departure*: "14 December 1941. Pupil has run away."

It was a Sunday. I imagine she would have taken advantage of the free day to visit her parents. That evening, she failed to return to the convent.

Those dying weeks of the year were the blackest, most claustrophobic period that Paris had known since the beginning of the Occupation. Between 8 and 14 December, in reprisal for two assassination attempts, the Germans ordered a curfew from six o'clock at night. Next came the round-up of 700 French Jews on 12 December; and the fine of one billion francs levied on the Jewish community as a whole. And then, on the morning of the same day, the shooting of seventy hostages at Mont Valérien. On

10 December, by order of the Prefect of Police, French and foreign Jews living in the département of the Seine had to submit to "periodic checks", producing special identity cards stamped "Jew" or "Jewess". Henceforth they were forbidden to travel outside the département and any change of address had to be registered with the police within twenty-four hours.

In parts of the 18th arrondissement, a curfew imposed by the Germans had been in force since 1 December. Nobody could enter the area after six o'clock at night. Local métro stations were closed, including Simplon, the one nearest to where Ernest and Cécile Bruder lived. A hand grenade had been thrown in the Rue Championnet, very close to their hotel.

*

The curfew lasted three days. It had no sooner been lifted than the Germans imposed another throughout the entire 10th arrondissement, where, on the Boulevard Magenta, persons unknown had fired at an officer of the occupying authorities. Then came the general curfew of 8 to 14 December – the Sunday of Dora's escape.

As the lights were extinguished district by district the town around the Convent of The Holy Heart of Mary became a dark prison. While Dora was behind the high walls of 60–62 Rue de Picpus, her parents were confined to their hotel room.

Her father having failed to declare her a "Jewess" in October 1940, she had not been alloted a "Jewish dossier" number. But the decree pertaining to the register of Jews issued by the Prefecture of Police on 10 December had stipulated that "subsequent changes in the family situation must be notified". I doubt that Dora's father would have had either the time or the inclination to get her inscribed on a file before she ran away. He must have thought that as long as she remained at the Holy Heart of Mary, her existence would never be suspected by the Prefecture of Police.

What makes us decide to run away? I remember my own flight on 18 January 1960, at a period which had none of the blackness of December 1941. My escape route, which took me past the hangars of Villacoublay airfield, had only one point in common with Dora's, namely, the season: winter. A calm, ordinary winter, not to be compared with that eighteen years earlier. But it seems that the sudden urge to escape may be prompted by one of those cold, grey days which makes you more than ever aware of your solitude, intensifying your feeling that a trap is about to close.

*

Sunday 14 December was the first day that the curfew had been lifted for almost a week. People were now free to go out after six o'clock in the evening. But because of German Time,* darkness fell in the afternoon.

At what moment of the day did the Sisters of Divine Mercy first notice that Dora was missing? It is certain to have been evening. Perhaps after Sunday Prayers in the chapel, as the boarders went upstairs to the dormitory. I expect the Mother Superior tried to reach Dora's parents at once, to find out if she was still with them. Was she aware that Dora and her parents were Jewish? According to her biographical note: "Many children from the families of persecuted Jews found refuge in the Holy Heart of Mary, thanks to the courageous and charitable actions of Sister Marie-Jean-Baptiste. Supported in these by the discreet and no less courageous attitude of her nuns, she shrank from nothing, whatever the risk."

But Dora's case was different. The persecutions had not yet begun in May 1940, when she entered the Holy Heart of Mary. She had missed the census in October 1940. And it was not till July 1942, after the great round-up, that religious institutions began to hide Jewish children. She had been at the Convent of The Holy Heart of Mary for a year and a half. In all likelihood, she was its sole Jewish pupil. Was this common knowledge among the nuns, among her fellow-boarders?

The Café Marchal on the ground floor of the hotel at

* The occupying authorities had brought the clocks forward by one hour to correspond with German Reich Time. See Pryce-Jones, *op. cit.*

41 Boulevard Ornano had a telephone: Montmartre 44–74; but I don't know if it had a line to the hotel, which may or may not have been owned by Marchal. The Convent of The Holy Heart of Mary is not listed in the telephone directory for the period. I have found a separate address for the Sisters of the Christian Schools of Divine Mercy, which in 1942 must have been an annexe to the convent: 64 Rue Saint-Maur. Did Dora ever go there? It too had no telephone number.

Who knows? The Mother Superior may have waited till Monday morning before telephoning the Café Marchal or, as is more likely, sending a nun to 41 Boulevard Ornano. Unless Cécile and Ernest Bruder went to the convent themselves.

It would help to know if the weather was fine on 14 December, the day of Dora's escape. Perhaps it was one of those mild, sunny winter days when you have a feeling of holiday and eternity – the illusion that the passage of time is suspended, and that you need only slip through this breach to escape the trap which is closing around you.

For a long time, I knew nothing about Dora Bruder after her escape on 14 December and the appearance of the missing notice in *Paris Soir*. Then I learnt that, eight months later, on 13 August 1942, she had been interned in the camp at Drancy. On the file, it stated that she had come from Tourelles camp. That 13 August, in fact, 300 Jewish women were transferred from Tourelles to Drancy.

Tourelles prison "camp", or rather, internment centre, occupied former colonial infantry barracks at 11 Boulevard Mortier, near the Porte des Lilas. It had been opened in October 1940 for the internment of foreign Jews whose situation was deemed "irregular". But after 1941, while men were sent directly to Drancy, or to camps in the Loiret, only Jewish women considered to have contravened German regulations were interned in Tourelles, together with women who were Communists or common criminals.

When, and for what precise reasons, was Dora Bruder sent to Tourelles? I wondered if there were not some existing document, some trace to provide me with the answer. For this, I was reduced to guesswork. She was probably arrested in the street. In February 1942 – two months after her escape – the Germans had issued a decree forbidding Jews to change address or to leave home after eight o'clock at night. Surveillance in the streets was thus stricter than in preceding months. In the end, I persuaded myself that Dora had been picked up during that dismal, icy-cold February when the Jewish Affairs police* had set their ambushes in the corridors of the métro, at the entrances to cinemas or the exits of theatres. In fact, it astonished me that a sixteen-year-old girl, whose description and disappearance in December were known to the police, had managed to elude her captors for so long. Unless she had found a hide-out. But where, in that Paris winter of 1941–42, the darkest and most severe of the Occupation, with snow from November onwards, a temperature of -15ºC in January, frozen puddles and black ice everywhere and more heavy snowfalls in February? What refuge could she have found? And how did she manage to survive in a Paris like that?

It would have been February, I imagine, when "they" had caught her in their net. "They" could as easily have

* The P.Q.J., *Police aux Questions Juives*, established in November 1941.

56

been uniformed men on the beat as inspectors from the Brigade for the Protection of Minors* or the Jewish Affairs police, carrying out an identity check in a public place ... In a book of memoirs, I had read that eighteen and nineteen-year-old girls, and even some as young as sixteen, Dora's age, had been sent to Tourelles for trivial infringements of "German laws". That same February, on the evening the German decree came into force, my father was caught in a round-up on the Champs Élysées. Inspectors of the Jewish Affairs police had blocked the exits from a restaurant in the Rue de Marignan where he was dining with a girlfriend. They had asked everybody for their papers. My father carried none. He was arrested. In the Black Maria taking them from the Champs Élysées to P.Q.J. headquarters in the Rue Greffulhe, he noticed, among the other shadowy figures, a young girl of about eighteen. He had lost sight of her as they were being hustled up to the first floor of this police den, where its chief, a certain Superintendent Schweblin, had his office. Then, taking advantage of a light on a time-switch that went out just as he was being escorted downstairs to be taken to the Dépôt,† he succeeded in making his escape.

My father had barely mentioned this young girl when, for the first and only time in his life, one night in June 1963, he told me about his narrow escape as we were dining in

* *Brigade des mineurs*.
† Temporary detention centre in the Prefecture of Police.

a restaurant off the Champs Élysées almost opposite the one where he had been arrested twenty years before. He gave me no details about her looks or clothes, and I had all but forgotten her until the day I learned of Dora Bruder's existence. Then, suddenly remembering the presence of this young girl among the other unknowns with my father in the Black Maria on that February night, it occured to me that she might have been Dora Bruder, that she too had just been arrested and was about to be sent to Tourelles.

Perhaps I wanted them to have met, she and my father, in that winter of 1942. Utterly different though they were, both, that winter, had found themselves in the same category, classed as outlaws. My father, too, had missed the census in October 1940, and, like Dora Bruder, had no "Jewish dossier" number. Consequently, no longer having any legal existence, he had cut all threads with a world where you were nothing without a job, a family, a nationality, a date of birth, an address. Henceforth he was in limbo. Not unlike Dora, after her escape.

But on reflection, their respective fates were very different. There were few courses of action open to a sixteen-year-old girl left to fend for herself, in Paris, in the winter of 1942, after having escaped from a convent. In the eyes of the police and the authorities of that time, her situation was doubly "irregular": she was not only Jewish, she was a minor on the run.

For my father, who was fourteen years older than Dora Bruder, the way was already mapped out: since they had made him an outlaw, he had had no choice but to follow that same course, to live on his wits in Paris and vanish into the swamps of the black market.

*

Not long ago, I discovered that the girl in the Black Maria could not have been Dora Bruder. I was looking for her name on the list of women who had been interned in Tourelles camp. Of these, two, Polish Jews aged twenty and twenty-one, had entered Tourelles on 18 and 19 February 1942. Their names were Syma Berger and Fredel Traister. The dates fitted, but was she in fact either girl? After passing through the Dépôt, the men were sent to the camp at Drancy, the women to Tourelles. Perhaps, like my father, the unknown girl had escaped the common fate in store for them both. I believe that she will remain forever anonymous, like all those shadowy figures arrested that night. The Jewish Affairs police having destroyed their own files, there are no records of arrests made during a round-up, nor of individuals picked up on the street. Were I not here to record it, there would be no trace of this unidentified girl's presence, nor of my father's, in a Black Maria on the Champs Élysées in February 1942. Nothing but those individuals – living or dead – officially classed as "person unknown".

Twenty years later, my mother was acting in a play at the Théâtre Michel. Often, I would wait for her in a café on the corner of the Rue des Mathurins and the Rue Greffulhe. I didn't know then that my father had risked his life near there, nor that I had entered a zone that was once a black hole. We would dine in a restaurant on the Rue Greffulhe – it may have been the ground floor of the P.Q.J. building where my father had been hustled into Superintendent Schweblin's office. Jacques Schweblin. Born 1901, Mulhouse. It was his men, at the camps of Drancy and Pithiviers, who had undertaken the search of internees prior to each departure for Auschwitz:

"M. Schweblin, head of the P.Q.J., would arrive at the camp accompanied by three or four aides whom he identified as 'auxiliaries', giving nobody's name but his own. Each of these plain-clothes policemen wore a uniform belt with a pistol hanging from one side and a truncheon from the other.

Once he had installed his aides, M. Schweblin would leave the camp, returning only in the evening to collect the fruits of their search. Each aide would set himself up in a hut containing a table and, beside it, two receptacles, one for cash, the other for jewellery. The internees then filed past the men, who would then subject them to a minute and humiliating search. Very often they were beaten, or forced to remove their trousers and submit to a hard kicking, accompanied by remarks like: 'Hey you! Want another taste of the police boot?' Frequently, on the pretext of expediting the search, inside and outside pockets would simply be torn off. I will pass over the intimate body-searches suffered by the women.

The search finished, cash and jewellery would be piled anyhow into boxes that were bound with string and sealed before being loaded into M. Schweblin's car.

This process was a farce, given that the sealing-tongs were in the hands of the policemen, who were free to help themselves to banknotes and jewels. In fact, these men would openly produce a valuable ring from their pockets, saying: 'Hey, that's not bad!', or a fistful of 1000 or 500-franc notes, saying, 'Hey, I forgot this.' Bedding in the huts was also searched: mattresses, eiderdowns and bolsters were ripped open. Of all the many searches performed by the Jewish Affairs police, not a single trace remains." *

* Extract from an official report drawn up in November 1943 by a manager from Pithiviers tax office.

The search team always consisted of the same seven men. Plus one woman. Their names are unknown. They were young at the time, so some must still be alive today. But their faces would be unrecognizable.

Schweblin disappeared in 1943. The Germans disposed of him themselves. Yet when my father was telling me about being taken to this man's office, he said that he was positive that he had recognized him at the Porte Maillot, one Sunday after the war.

Black Marias remained much the same till the early 1960s. The only time in my life that I have found myself in one was with my father, and I wouldn't mention it now had this episode not taken on a symbolic character for me.

The circumstances were banal in the extreme. I was eighteen years old, still a minor. My parents, though separated, had continued to live in the same block, my father with a very highly-strung woman whose hair was the colour of straw, a sort of imitation Mylène Demongeot. And I with my mother. That day, on the landing, a quarrel had broken out between my parents about the very modest sum which my father had been ordered to pay for my maintenance following a series of judicial proceedings: High Court of the Seine. Court of Appeal, 1st Auxiliary Chamber. Notification of Judgment to the party concerned. My mother had asked me to ring at his door and demand this money, which he had failed to hand over. Unfortunately, it was all we had to live on. I did so with reluctance. When I rang my father's bell I meant to ask him nicely, even to apologize for bothering him. He slammed the door in my face; I could hear the pseudo-Mylène Demongeot on the telephone to the police emergency service, screaming something about "a young hooligan making a scene".

They came for me at my mother's about ten minutes later, and my father and I climbed into the waiting Black Maria. We sat facing one another, on wooden benches, each flanked by two policemen. I thought to myself that while it was the first time in my life that something like this had happened to me, my father had been through it all before, on that February night twenty years ago when the Jewish Affairs police had taken him away in a van much like this one. And I wondered if, at that moment, he was thinking the same thing. But he avoided my eyes, pretending to ignore me.

I remember every minute of that drive. The embankments along the Seine. The Rue des Saint-Pères. The Boulevard Saint-Germain. The stop at the lights opposite the Café des Deux Magots. I peered enviously through the barred windows at the drinkers sitting on the terrace in the sun. Luckily, I had little to worry about: we were in that anodyne, innocuous period later known as the "Thirty Glorious Years".[*]

Yet I was surprised that, after all he had been through during the Occupation, my father should not have offered the slightest objection to my being taken away in a Black Maria. Sitting there, opposite me, impassive, with an air of faint disgust, he ignored me as if I had the plague, and I dreaded our arrival at the police station, knowing that I could expect no sympathy from him. I felt the injustice of this all the more since I had embarked on a book – my first – in which, putting myself in his place, I relived his anguish during the Occupation. A few years earlier, among his books, I had come across certain anti-Semitic works from the 1940s which he must have bought at the time in an effort to understand what it was that these writers had against him. And I can well imagine his surprise at the portrayal of this imaginary, phantasmagoric monster with claw-like hands and hooked nose whose shadow flitted across the walls, this creature corrupted by every vice, responsible for every ill, guilty of every crime. As for me, I wanted my first book to be a riposte to all those who, by insulting my father, had wounded me; to silence them once and for all on the field of French prose. I can see now that my plan was childishly naïve: most of the authors were gone, executed by firing squad, exiled, senile or dead of old age. Yes, alas, I was too late.

[*] "*Les Trentes Glorieuses*", an expression for the years of post-war boom in France.

The Black Maria drew up in the Rue de l'Abbaye outside the Saint-Germain-des-Prés police station. Our guards led us into the superintendent's office. Crisply, my father informed him that I was a "young hooligan" and had been "making scenes" in his house since I was sixteen years old. To me, the superintendent said that he would "take me in if there was a next time", in the tone of voice you use to a delinquent. I had the distinct impression that if the superintendent had carried out his threat and sent me to the Dépôt, my father wouldn't have lifted a finger to help.

My father and I left the police station together. I asked him if it was really necessary to call the police emergency service and have me "booked" in front of everybody. He didn't answer me. I bore him no grudge. Since we lived in the same building, we walked back the same way side by side, in silence. I was tempted to remind him of that night in February 1942 when he too had been taken away in a Black Maria, to ask him whether he had been thinking of that, just now. But perhaps it meant less to him than it did to me.

On the way home, we didn't exchange a single word, not even when we parted on the staircase. I was to see him once or twice in August of the following year, on an occasion when he hid my call-up papers as a ruse to have me carted off by force to the Reuilly army barracks. After that I never saw him again.

What did Dora Bruder do first, I wonder, once she had made her escape on 14 December 1941. Perhaps she had decided not to return to the convent the instant she had arrived at the gate, and had spent the evening wandering the streets till curfew.

Streets which still had countrified names: Les Meuniers, La Brèche-aux-Loups, Le sentier des Merisiers. But at the top of the little tree-shaded street which ran alongside the perimeter wall of the Holy Heart of Mary there was a goods yard, and further on, if you take the Avenue Daumesnil, the Gare de Lyon. The railway tracks to this station pass within a few hundred metres of the convent in which Dora Bruder had been shut up. This peaceful quarter, which feels so far from Paris, with its convents, its hidden cemeteries and quiet avenues, is also a point of departure.

I don't know if it was the proximity of the Gare de Lyon that had encouraged Dora to run away. Whether, from her dormitory in the silence of the black-out, she could hear the rattle of freight cars or the sound of trains leaving the Gare de Lyon for the Free Zone ... She was doubtless familiar with those two duplicitous words: Free Zone.

In the novel I had written at a time when I knew almost nothing about Dora Bruder but wanted to keep her in the forefront of my mind, the girl of her age whom I called Ingrid hides in the Free Zone with her boyfriend. I was thinking of Bella D. who, at the age of fifteen, had also smuggled herself out of Paris across the demarcation line, only to end up in a Toulouse prison; of Anne B., who was picked up without a travel-permit on Chalon-sur-Saône station and sentenced to twelve weeks in prison ... These are things that they had told me about in the 1960s.

Did Dora Bruder prepare her escape long in advance, with the complicity of a friend, boy or girl? Did she remain in Paris, or did she in fact try to reach the Free Zone?

The logbook at Clignancourt police station has this entry for 27 December 1941 under columns headed: *Date and subject. Marital status. Summary.*

27 December 1941. Bruder, Dora, born Paris 12, 25/2/26, living at 41 Boulevard Ornano. Interview with Bruder, Ernest, age 42, father.

The following figures are written in the margin, but I have no idea what they stand for: 7029 21/12.

The superintendent at Clignancourt police station, 12 Rue Lambert, behind the Butte Montmartre, was called Siri. But Ernest Bruder probably went to the divisional station, 74 Rue du Mont-Cenis, next to the Town Hall, which was also part of the Clignancourt district: it was nearer his home. The superintendent there was called Cornec.

Dora had run away thirteen days earlier, and Ernest Bruder had waited all that time then before notifying the police of his daughter's disappearance. His anguish and indecision during those long thirteen days can be imagined. The police station was the one where he had been supposed to register Dora at the time of the census in October 1940, and the omission would probably be noticed. By trying to find her, he was drawing attention to her.

The transcript of Ernest Bruder's interview is missing from the Prefecture of Police archives. No doubt local police stations destroyed such documents as they became redundant. Other police records were destroyed, a few years after the war, such as the special registers opened during the week in June 1942 when every Jewish person over the age of six was issued with three yellow stars. These registers, which had a column in the margin where you signed on receipt of your stars, recorded your civil status, identity card number and place of domicile. Police stations in Paris and the suburbs compiled over fifty such registers.

We shall never know how Ernest Bruder answered the questions put to him about his daughter and himself. Perhaps he chanced upon a desk clerk for whom it was a matter of routine, like before the war, and who saw no particular difference between Ernest Bruder and his daughter and ordinary French citizens. To be sure, the man was an "ex-Austrian", and an unskilled labourer living in a hotel. But his daughter was born in Paris and had French nationality. A runaway adolescent. It happened more and more in these troubled times. Did this policeman advise Ernest Bruder to put the missing notice in *Paris Soir*, given that almost two weeks had passed since Dora's disappearance? Or did a *Paris Soir* reporter, touring the police stations in search of "fillers", happen to see it among other incidents of the day and glean it for the paper's "From Day to Day" columns?

*

I remember the intensity of my feelings while I was on the run in January 1960 – an intensity such as I have seldom known. It was the intoxication of cutting all ties at a stroke: the clean, deliberate break, with enforced rules, boarding school, teachers, classmates. From now on you need have nothing to do with them; the break with your parents, who have never understood you and to whom, you tell yourself, it is useless turning for help; feelings of rebellion and solitude, carried to incandescence, taking your breath away and leaving you in a state of weightlessness. It was probably one of the few times in my life when I was truly myself and following my own bent.

This ecstasy cannot last. It has no future. Your high spirits are soon shattered for good.

Running away – it seems – is a call for help and

occasionally a form of suicide. At least you experience a moment of eternity. You have broken your ties not only with the world but also with time. And one fine morning you find that the sky is light blue and there is nothing to weigh you down. In the Tuileries gardens, the hands on the clock have stopped for good. An ant is transfixed in its journey across a patch of sunlight.

*

I think of Dora Bruder. I remind myself that, for her, running away was not as easy as it was for me, twenty years later, in a world that had once again been rendered harmless. To her, everything in that city of December 1941, its curfews, its soldiers, its police, was hostile, intent on her destruction. At nearly sixteen years old, without knowing why, she had the entire world against her.

Other rebels in the Paris of those years, equally solitary, were throwing hand grenades at the Germans, into their convoys and meeting places. They were her age. Some of their faces appeared on the Affiche Rouge,* and, I cannot help associating them in my mind with Dora.

In the summer of 1941, a film made under the Occupation which had opened in Normandy came to the local Paris cinemas. It was a harmless comedy: *Premier rendez-vous*. The last time I saw it, I had a strange feeling that

* "Wanted" posters, printed in red, put up by the Germans, serving death-notices. See Pryce-Jones, *op. cit.*

was out of keeping with the thin plot and the sprightly tones of the actors. I told myself that perhaps, one Sunday, Dora Bruder had been to see this film, the subject of which was a girl of her age who runs away. She escapes from a boarding school, like the Holy Heart of Mary. During her flight, as in fairy tales and romances, she meets her Prince Charming.

This film paints a rosy, anodyne picture of what happened to Dora in real life. Did it give her the idea of running away? I concentrated on details: the dormitory, the school corridors, the boarders' uniforms, the café where the heroine waits after dark . . . I could find nothing which might correspond to the reality, and in any case most of the scenes were shot in the studio. And yet, I had a sense of unease. It stemmed from the film's peculiar luminosity, from the grain of the actual film-stock. Every image seemed veiled in an arctic whiteness which accentuated the contrasts and sometimes obliterated them. The lighting was at once too bright and too dim, either stifling the voices or giving them a louder, more disturbing timbre.

Suddenly, I realised that this film was impregnated with the gaze of cinema goers from the time of the Occupation – people from all walks of life, most of whom would not have survived the war. They had been taken out of themselves after having seen this film one Saturday night, their night out. While it lasted, you forgot the

73

war and the menacing world outside. Huddled together in the dark of a cinema, you were caught up in the flow of images on the screen, and nothing more could happen to you. And, by some chemical process, this combined gaze had altered the very substance of the film, the lighting, the voices of the actors. That is what I had sensed, thinking of Dora Bruder and watching the ostensibly trivial images of *Premier rendez-vous*.

Ernest Bruder was arrested on 19 March 1942, or to be precise, that was the day he was interned at Drancy. I have been unable to find any trace of the circumstances of his arrest, nor of the reasons for it. In one of the so-called "family files" that contained a few basic facts about each individual Jew and which were held at the Prefecture of Police, his entry reads:

Bruder, Ernest
21.5.99 – Vienna
Jewish dossier no: 49091
Trade or profession: None
French legionnaire, 2nd class. 100% disabled. Gassed;
    pulmonary tuberculosis
Central police register E56404

Lower down, the file is stamped WANTED, next to which somebody has pencilled the words: "Traced to Drancy camp".

As a Jew and an "ex-Austrian", Ernest Bruder could have been arrested in the round-up of August 1941, during which the French police, supported by the German army, cordoned off the 11th arrondissement on 20 August and then, in the days that followed, stopped and questioned foreign Jews in the streets of other arrondissements, including the 18th. How had he escaped this round-up? Thanks to his rank as an ex-French legionnaire, 2nd class? I doubt it.

According to his file, he was "wanted". But since when? And why, exactly? If he was already "wanted" on 27 December 1941, the day he had notified the Clignancourt police of Dora's disappearance, he wouldn't have been allowed to leave the police station. Did he draw attention to himself on that day?

A father tries to find his daughter, notifies her disappearance at a police station, and a missing notice is inserted in an evening newspaper. But the father himself is "wanted". The parents lose all trace of their daughter and, on 19 March, one of them disappears in their turn, as if the winter that year was cutting people off from one another, muddying and wiping out their tracks to the point where their existence is in doubt. And there is no redress. The very people whose job it is to search for you are themselves compiling dossiers, the better to ensure that, once found, you will disappear again – this time for good.

I don't know if Dora Bruder learned of her father's arrest at once. I imagine not. By March, she had still not returned to 41 Boulevard Ornano after her escape in December. Or so it would seem from such traces of her as survive in the Prefecture of Police archives.

Now that almost sixty years have elapsed, these archives will gradually reveal their secrets. All that remains of the building occupied by the Prefecture of Police during the Occupation is the huge spectral barracks beside the Seine. It reminds us a little, whenever we evoke the past, of The House of Usher. And we can hardly believe that this building we pass every day is unchanged since the 1940s. We persuade ourselves that these cannot be the same stones, the same corridors.

The superintendents and inspectors who hunted down the Jews are long dead, and their names have a sombre

78

ring, and give off a smell of rotting leather and stale tobacco: Permilleux, François, Schweblin, Koerperich, Cougoule ... Also dead, or far gone in senility, are the street police, known to us as the "press gang", who signed the transcript of every interview with those whom they arrested during the round-ups. Every one of those tens of thousands of transcripts has been destroyed, and we shall never know the identity of the members of the "press gang". But there remain, in the archives, hundreds and hundreds of letters addressed to the Prefect of Police of the day, to which he never replied. They have been there for over half a century, like sacks of air mail lying forgotten in the recesses of a remote hangar. Now we can read them. Those to whom they were addressed having ignored them, it is we, who were not even born at the time, who are their recipients and their guardians:

To the Prefect of Police
Sir,

I humbly draw your attention to my request. It concerns my nephew Albert Graudens, a French citizen, aged sixteen, who has been interned at ...

To the Director of the Police for Jewish Affairs
Sir,

I implore you to have the great kindness to release my daughter Nelly Trautmann from Drancy camp ...

To the Prefect of Police
Sir,

I venture to ask you a favour in respect of my husband, Zelik Pergricht, so that I may know how he is and have a little news . . .

To the Prefect of Police
Sir,

I humbly beg you in your great kindness and generosity for news of my daughter, Mme Jacques Lévy, *née* Violette Joel, arrested about 10 September last as she was trying to cross the demarcation line without wearing the regulation star. She was accompanied by her son, Jean Lévy, aged eight and a half . . .

Forwarded to the Prefect of Police

I beg you to have the kindness to release my grandson, Michel Robin, aged three, French-born of a French mother, who is interned with him at Drancy . . .

To the Prefect of Police

I would be infinitely grateful if you would be good enough to take the following cases into consideration: my parents, both elderly and in poor health, have just been arrested as Jews, and my little sister, Marie Grosman, aged twelve and a half, a French Jew, holding French identity-card no. 1594936, grade B, and myself, Jeanette Grosman, also a French Jew, aged nineteen, the holder of French identity-card no. 924247, grade B, have been left on our own ...

To the Director of the Police for Jewish Affairs
Sir,

Excuse me if I presume to write to you in person about this, but my husband was taken away at 4 a.m. on 16 July 1942, and as my little girl was crying, they took her at the same time.

Her name is Pauline Gothelf, aged fourteen and a half, born 19 November 1927 in Paris, 12th arrondissement, and she is French ...

For the date of 17 April 1942, the logbook at Clignancourt police station has this entry under the usual headings: *Date and subject. Marital status. Summary.*

> 17 April 1942. 20998 15/24. P. Minors. Case of Bruder, Dora, age 16, disappeared following Interview 1917. Has regained maternal domicile.

I don't know what the figures 20998 and 15/24 stand for. "P. Minors" must mean Protection of Minors. Interview 1917 is certainly the transcript of Ernest Bruder's deposition, and the questions concerning Dora and himself which were put to him on 27 December 1941. This is the sole reference in the archives to Interview 1917.

A bare three lines on the "case of Bruder, Dora". The entries which come after it in the logbook for 17 April concern other "cases":

Gaul Georgette Paulette, born 30.7.23 Pantin, Seine, to Georges and Pelz Rose, spinster, living in hotel 11 Rue Pigalle. Prostitution.

Germaine Mauraire, born 9.10.21 Entre-Deux-Eaux (Vosges). Living in hotel. 1 P.M. report."*

J.-R. Cretet, 9th arrondissement.

So the list goes on, throughout the Occupation, in police station logbooks: prostitutes, lost dogs, abandoned babies. And runaway adolescents – like Dora – guilty of vagrancy.

Apparently, "Jews" as such never came into it. And yet they passed through these same police stations before being taken to the Dépôt, and from there to Drancy. And the phrase "regained maternal domicile" suggests that the Clignancourt police were aware that Dora's father had been arrested the month before.

Of Dora herself, there is no trace between 14 December 1941, the day she ran away, and 17 April 1942 when, in the words of the logbook, she regained the maternal domicile, that is, the hotel room at 41 Boulevard Ornano. For those four months, we have no idea where she went, what she did, whom she was with. Nor do we know the circumstances of her return to the "maternal domicile". Was it of her own accord, after having heard of her father's

* Allusion to a report by the *Police des Moeurs*, or Vice Squad.

arrest? Or had she in fact been stopped in the street, the Brigade for the Protection of Minors having issued a warrant for her arrest? So far, I haven't found a single clue, a single witness who might shed light on these four months of absence which, for us, remain a blank in her life.

One way not to lose all touch with Dora Bruder over this period would be to report on the changes in the weather. The first snow fell on 4 November 1941. Winter got off to a cold start on 22 December. On 29 December, the thermometer dropped still lower and a thin coating of ice formed on the windowpanes. From 13 January onwards, the cold became Siberian. Water froze. This lasted some four weeks. On 12 February, the sun came out briefly, like a tentative annunciation of spring. The snow on the pavements, trampled by pedestrians, turned to a dirty slush. It was on the evening of 12 February that my father was picked up by the Jewish Affairs police. On 22 February, it snowed again. On 25 February, there was a fresh, much heavier snowfall. On 3 March, just after 9 p.m., the first bombs fell on the suburbs. Windows rattled in Paris. On 13 March, in broad daylight, the sirens sounded a general alert. Passengers were stuck in the métro for two hours. They were led out through the tunnel. A second alert that same day, at 10 p.m. 15 March was a beautiful sunny day. On 28 March, about 10 p.m., a distant air raid, lasting till midnight. On 2 April, around 4 a.m., an alert, followed by a heavy bombardment till

6. More raids from 11 p.m. On 4 April, the buds on the chestnut trees burst open. On 5 April, towards evening, a passing spring storm brought hail and, with it, a rainbow. Don't forget: rendezvous tomorrow afternoon, on the terrace of the Café-des Gobelins.

A few months ago, I managed to get hold of a photograph of Dora Bruder which is in complete contrast to those already in my collection. It may be the last ever taken of her. Her face and demeanour have none of the childlike qualities which shine out from the earlier photographs, in the gaze, the rounded cheeks, the white dress worn on a prize day ... I don't know when this photograph was taken. It could only have been in 1941, when Dora was a boarder at the Holy Heart of Mary, or else early in the spring of 1942, when she returned to the Boulevard Ornano after her escape in December.

She is with her mother and her maternal grandmother. The three women are side by side, the grandmother between Cécile Bruder and Dora. Cécile Bruder, her hair cut short, wears black, the grandmother's dress is flowered. Neither woman is smiling. Dora wears a two-piece dress in black – or navy-blue – with a white collar, but this could equally well be a cardigan and skirt – the photograph is too dark to see. She is wearing stockings and ankle-strap shoes. Her mid-length hair, held back by a headband, falls almost to her shoulders, her left arm hangs down at her side, fingers clenched, her right arm is hidden behind her grandmother. She holds her head high, her eyes are grave but the beginnings of a smile floats about her lips. And this gives her face an expression of sad sweetness and defiance. The three women are standing in front of a wall. The ground is paved, as in the passage of some public place. Who could have been the photographer? Ernest Bruder? Or does the fact that he is not present in the photograph mean that he had already been arrested? In any case, it would seem that the three women have put on their Sunday best to face this anonymous lens.

Could it be that Dora is wearing the navy-blue skirt mentioned in the missing persons notice in *Paris Soir*?

*

Such photographs exist in every family. They were caught in a few seconds, the duration of the exposure, and these seconds have become an eternity.

Why, one wonders, does lightning strike in one place rather than another? Suddenly, as I write these lines, I find myself thinking of former colleagues in my profession. Today, I am visited by the memory of a German writer. His name was Fredo Lampe.

It was his name that first caught my attention, and the title of one of his books, *Am Rande der Nacht*, translated into French some twenty years ago, about the time I came across it in a bookshop on the Champs Élysées. I had never heard of this writer. But even before opening the book, I had divined its tone and atmosphere, as though I had already read him in another life.

Fredo Lampe. *Am Rande der Nacht.* For me, name and title evoked those lighted windows from which you cannot tear your gaze. You are convinced that, behind them, somebody whom you have forgotten has been awaiting your return for years, or else that there is no longer anybody there. Only a lamp, left burning in the empty room.

Fredo Lampe was born in Bremen in 1899, the same year as Ernest Bruder. He had gone to Heidelberg university. He had begun *Am Rande der Nacht,* his first novel, in Hamburg, where he worked as a librarian. Later, he took a job with a publisher in Berlin. He had no interest in politics. His passion was for writing about the port of Bremen at nightfall, the lilac-white of the floodlights, the sailors, the wrestlers, the bands, the whistling of the trains, the railway bridge, the ships' sirens, and all those who seek out their fellow beings at night . . . His novel appeared in October 1933, by which time Hitler was already in power. *Am Rande der Nacht* was withdrawn from the shops and pulped, and its author declared "suspect". He was not even Jewish. To what, then, could they possibly have objected? Quite simply, to the charm and nostalgia of his book. His one ambition – he confided in a letter – was "to bring alive the surroundings of a port for a few hours in the evening, between eight o'clock and midnight. I'm thinking here of the Bremen district where I grew up. Of short scenes unfolding as in a film, interlocking people's lives. The whole thing light and fluid, linked together very loosely, pictorial, lyric, full of atmosphere."

Towards the end of the war, at the time of the advance of the Russian troops, he was living in a Berlin suburb. On 2 May 1945, he was stopped in the street by two Russian soldiers who asked him for his papers, then dragged him into a park. And there, without having taken the time to distinguish between the good and wicked, they beat him to death. Some neighbours buried him nearby, in the shade of a birch tree, and arranged for the police to receive his remains: his papers and his hat.

*

Like Fredo Lampe, the German writer Felix Hartlaub was a native of the port of Bremen. He was born in 1913. During the Occupation he found himself in Paris. He had a horror of this war, and of his grey-green uniform. I know very little about him. In a 1950s magazine, I read, in translation, an extract from a short book of his, *Von Unten Gesehen*, the manuscript of which he had entrusted to his sister in January 1945. The extract was entitled "*Notes et Impressions*". In it, he observes the crowd in a typical Paris station-buffet, and the abandoned Ministry of Foreign Affairs as it was when the Germans moved in, with its hundreds of empty, dusty offices, the chandeliers left burning and the clocks all chiming incessantly in the silence. At night, so as to forget the war and merge with the Paris streets, he puts on civilian clothes. He gives us an account of one of these nocturnal excursions. He takes the métro from Solférino. He gets out at Trinité. The night is dark. It is summer. The air is warm. He walks up the Rue de Clichy in the black-out. On a sofa, in a brothel, he sees a solitary, pathetic Tyrolean hat. The girls file past. "They are in another world, like sleepwalkers under the effects of chloroform. And everything is bathed" – he writes – "in the eerie light of a tropical aquarium under overheated glass." He too is in another world. He observes everything from a distance, attentive to atmosphere, to every tiny, mundane detail, and at the same time he is detached, estranged from everything around him, as though this world at war was no concern of his. Like Fredo Lampe, he died in Berlin, aged thirty-three, during the final battles of spring 1945, amid the carnage of an apocalyptic world in which he had found himself by mistake, wearing a uniform that had been imposed on him but which was not his own.

*

And now, why is it that, among so many other writers, my thoughts should turn to the poet Roger Gilbert-Lecomte? He too was struck down, in the same period as the two previous writers, as though the few must serve as lightning conductors in order that others may be spared.

As it happens, our paths had crossed. When I was his age, like him I lived in the southern suburbs of Paris: Boulevard Brune, Rue d'Alésia, Hôtel Primavera, Rue de la Voie-Verte ... He was still there in 1938, living near the Porte d'Orléans with a German-Jewish girl, Ruth Kronenberg. Then, in 1939, still with her, he moved the short distance to the Plaisance district, to a studio at 16*bis* Rue Bardinet. The number of times I have taken those streets, without even knowing that Gilbert-Lecomte had been there before me ... And in 1965, on the Right Bank, in Montmartre, I would spend entire afternoons in a corner café on the Square Caulaincourt, unaware that Gilbert-Lecomte had also stayed there thirty years earlier, in a hotel off the Rue Caulaincourt: Montmartre 42–99 ...

About this time, I came across a doctor called Jean Puyaubert. I thought I had a shadow on my lung. To avoid doing National Service, I asked him for a certificate. He gave me an appointment at a clinic where he worked in the Place d'Alleray, and had me x-rayed: I had nothing on my lung, I wanted an exemption, and it wasn't as though there was a war on. It was simply that the prospect of barrack-life such as I had already been leading in various boarding schools from the ages of eleven to seventeen seemed to me unendurable.

I don't know what became of Dr Jean Puyaubert. Decades after I had been to see him, I learned that Roger

Gilbert-Lecomte had been one of his closest friends, and that the poet, when my age, had asked him a similar favour: a medical certificate confirming that he had had pleurisy – to exempt him from National Service.

Roger Gilbert-Lecomte . . . He had dragged out his last years in Paris, under the Occupation . . . In July 1942, on her way back from the beach at Collioure, in the Free Zone, his friend Ruth Kronenberg was arrested. She was deported in the transport of 11 September, a week before Dora Bruder. A twenty-year-old from Cologne, she had come to Paris some time in 1935 because of the racial laws. She liked poetry and the theatre. She had learnt to sew in order to make theatrical costumes. Almost at once, in the company of other artists in Montparnasse, she had met Roger Gilbert-Lecomte . . .

He continued to live alone in the studio in the Rue Bardinet. Then a Mme Firmat, who had the café opposite, took him in and looked after him. He was a shadow of his former self. In autumn 1942, he undertook several exhausting journeys across the suburbs to Bois-Colombes, where a Dr Bréavoine in the Rue des Aubépines gave him prescriptions which allowed him to obtain a little heroin. His comings and goings were noted. On 21 October 1942, he was arrested and imprisoned in the Santé, where he remained, in the infirmary, till 19 November. He was released with a summons to appear in court a month later, charged with "having, in Paris, Colombes,

Bois-Colombes, Asnières, in 1942, illegally and without due motive, bought and kept in his possession prohibited drugs: heroin, morphine, cocaine . . ."

For a while, in early 1943, he was in a clinic at Épernay, then Mme Firmat put him up in a room above her café. A girl to whom he had lent the studio in Rue Bardinet during his stay at the clinic, a student, had left behind a box of ampoules containing morphine which he eked out, drop by drop. I never discovered her name.

He died from tetanus on 13 December 1943, at Broussais Hospital, aged thirty-six. Before the war, he had published two collections of poems; one of these books was entitled *La Vie, l'Amour, la Mort, le Vide et le Vent*.

So many friends whom I never knew disappeared in 1945, the year I was born.

As a child, in the apartment at 15 Quai de Conti where my father had lived since 1942 – the same apartment which Maurice Sachs* had rented the year before – my room overlooked the courtyard. Maurice Sachs relates that he lent these rooms to a man called Albert, nicknamed "le Zébu".† And that he in turn had filled them with "young actors who dreamt of forming their own company, and with adolescents who were beginning to write". This "Zébu", Albert Schaky, had the same forename as my

* The writer and aesthete. Sachs's book *La Chasse à courre* describes his life as a black-marketeer in Paris under the Occupation.
† A *zébu* is a domestic ox with a muscular hump and sharp horns.

father, and like him, came from a family of Italian Jews in Salonika. And, like me exactly thirty years later, at the same age, he had published his first novel with Gallimard, in 1938, at the age of twenty-one, under the name François Vernet. He later joined the Resistance. The Germans arrested him. On the wall of Cell 218, Fresnes, second division, he wrote: "Zébu arrested 10.2.44. Three months on bread and water, interrogated 9–28 May, visited by doctor 8 June, two days after Allied landing."

He was deported from Compiègne camp on the transport of 2 July 1944, and died in Dachau in March 1945.

Thus, in the apartment where Sachs had carried on his gold trafficking and where, later on, under a false name, my father had hidden, "Zébu" had occupied my childhood bedroom. Just before I was born, he and others like him had accepted all the punishments meted out to them in order that we should suffer no more than pinpricks. I had already worked this out at the age of eighteen, while on that journey with my father in the Black Maria, a journey which was a harmless repetition, a parody, of other such journeys – in the same police vans and to the same police stations – but from which nobody had ever returned home, on foot, as I had on that occasion.

*

On 31 December, when, like today, it had grown dark very early, I remember paying Dr Ferdière a visit late in the afternoon. I was twenty-three years old, at a period of my life filled with anguish and uncertainty, and this man had shown me the greatest kindness. I vaguely knew that he had admitted Antonin Artaud to the psychiatric hospital in Rodez, where he had done his best to treat him.[*] But I remember that particular evening for a striking coincidence: I had given Dr Ferdière a copy of my first book, *La Place de l'Étoile*, the title of which surprised him. He took down a slim, grey volume from his bookshelves to show me: *La Place de l'Étoile* by Robert Desnos,[†] whose friend he was. Dr Ferdière had had it published himself, in Rodez, a few months after Desnos's death in the camp at Terezin in 1945, the year I was born. I had no idea that Desnos had written a book called *La Place de l'Étoile*. Quite unwittingly, I had stolen his title from him.

[*] Artaud, actor, poet, influential cineaste and theatrical pioneer, remained in Rodez asylum, in the Free Zone, until 1946; he died in 1948.
[†] A leading figure in Paris artistic circles, later active in the Resistance.

Two months ago, in the archives of the Yivo Institute, New York, a friend of mine found the following memo among documents relating to the former *Union Générale des Israélites de France,* [*] a body founded under the Occupation:

3L/SBL/   17 June 1942

0032

Memo to Mlle Salomon

Dora Bruder was restored to her mother on the 15th of this month, courtesy of the Clignancourt police.

In view of the fact that she has repeatedly run away, it would seem advisable to have her admitted

---

[*] In polite society, *Israélite* was used to avoid the connotations of the word "Jew".

to a remand home for juveniles.

The father being interned and the mother in a state of penury, police social workers (Quai de Gesvres) will take the necessary action if required.

Thus, after her return to the maternal domicile on 17 April 1942, Dora Bruder had run away a second time. We have no means of knowing for how long. A month, a month and a half stolen from the spring of 1942? A week? Where, and in what circumstances, had she been arrested and taken to Clignancourt police station?

From 7 June, the wearing of the yellow star had been mandatory. Jews whose names began with A and B had been collecting theirs at police stations since Tuesday 2 June, signing the registers opened for the purpose. Would Dora Bruder have been wearing the star when she was taken to the police station? I doubt it, remembering what her cousin had said about her. A rebel, independent-minded. And besides, in all likelihood she had been on the run long before the beginning of June.

Was she stopped in the street for not wearing the star? I have found the circular dated June 1942 setting out the penalties for those picked up for violation of the eighth statute[*] relating to the wearing of the insignia:

---

[*] The Vichy government had issued the first *statut des Juifs* in October 1940. Pryce-Jones, *op. cit.*

From the Directors of the Criminal Investigation Department and the Metropolitan Police

To Divisional Chief Superintendents, Traffic Commissioners for each arrondissement, Superintendents of Paris districts and all other metropolitan and criminal investigation departments (copies to: Directorates of Intelligence Services, Technical Services, Alien and Jewish Affairs...)

PROCEDURE

1 – Jews – males aged 18 and over:

Any Jew in breach of the law is to be remanded to the Dépôt by the Traffic Commissioner and furnished with a special and individual transfer warrant in duplicate (the second copy to Divisional Superintendent Roux, chief of the Motor Vehicles Department[*] – Dépôt unit), this document is to specify, in addition to the place, day, time and circumstances of the arrest, the name, forename, date and place of birth, family status, occupation, domicile and nationality of the statutory detainee.

2 – Jewish females and minors of both sexes aged between 16 and 18 years:

[*] Paris green buses had been comandeered for the transport of Jews. Pryce-Jones, *op.cit.*

The above are also to be remanded to the Dépôt by the Traffic Commissioner under the terms and conditions stated above.

Dépôt personnel are to send the original of the transfer warrant to the Directorate for Alien and Jewish Affairs, which will rule on each case after consultation with the German authorities. No release may be effected without written orders from the said directorate.

Directorate of Criminal Investigation

Tanguy

Directorate of Metropolitan Police

Hennequin

That June, hundreds of adolescents like Dora were arrested on the street in accordance with Tanguy's and Hennequin's precise and detailed instructions. They passed through the Dépôt and then Drancy on their way to Auschwitz. It goes without saying that the "special and individual traffic warrants" of which Superintendent Roux received copies were destroyed after the war, or even, perhaps, as each arrest was completed. Nevertheless, a few remain, inadvertently overlooked.

Police report dated 25 August 1942:
I am dispatching the following to the Dépôt for failure to wear the Jewish insignia: Sterman, Esther, born 13 June 1926, Paris 12th, domiciled

42 Rue des Francs-Bourgeois, 8th.

Rotsztein, Benjamin, born 19 December 1922, Warsaw, 5 Rue des Francs-Bourgeois, arrested Gare d'Austerlitz by inspectors of the Intelligence Service, Section 3.

Police report dated 1 September 1942:
From Inspectors Curinier and Lasalle to the Chief Superintendent, Special Brigade.

We are transferring to your custody Jacobson, Louise born Paris twelfth arrondissement twenty-four December nineteen hundred and twenty-four [. . .] naturalized French nineteen hundred and twenty-five, race Jewish, spinster. Domiciled with mother, 8 Rue des Boulets, eleventh arrondissement. Student.

Arrested today at approx. fourteen hundred hours at the maternal domicile in the following circumstances:

The Jacobson girl returned as we were proceeding with a domiciliary visit at the above address and we noted that she was not wearing the Jewish insignia in accordance with a German decree.

She states that she left home at eight thirty hours to study for her *baccalauréat* at the Lycée Henri IV, Rue Clovis.

However, the girl's neighbours informed us

that she frequently left home without wearing the insignia.

Neither we nor the Criminal Investigation Department have any record of the Jacobson girl in our files.

17 May 1944. Yesterday at 02.45h. two police officers from the 18th arrondissement arrested the French Jew Barmann, Jules, born 25 March 1925, Paris, 10th domiciled 40*bis* Rue du Ruisseau (18th) who being without the yellow star ran away on being questioned by the officers. Having fired three times in his direction without hitting him, the officers effected the arrest on the 8th floor of the apartment building at 12 Rue Charles-Nodier (18th) where he had taken refuge.

But according to the "Memo to Mlle Salomon", Dora Bruder had been returned to her mother. Whether or not she was wearing the star – her mother would have been wearing hers for at least a week – it means that, at Clignancourt police station, she was treated like any other runaway girl. Or it may be that the police themselves were responsible for the "Memo to Mlle Salomon".

I have been unable to trace Mlle Salomon. Is she still alive? Evidently, she was a member of U.G.I.F., the organisation administered by leading French Israelites who co-ordinated charity work among the Jewish community during the Occupation. Unfortunately, while the *Union Générale des Israélites de France* certainly came to the aid of a great many French Jews, its origins were ambiguous: it had been founded on the initiative of the Germans and the Vichy government on the assumption that control of such a body would facilitate their ends, as in the case of the *Judenräte* which they had set up in the towns and cities of Poland.

Both patrons and staff of the U.G.I.F. carried what was called a "legitimization card" to protect them from being rounded-up or interned. But this irregular privilege was soon to prove illusory. From 1943 onwards, leaders and employees of U.G.I.F. were arrested and deported in their hundreds. On a list of these I have found the name of an Alice Salomon, who had worked in the Free Zone. I don't think she can have been the Mlle Salomon to whom the memo about Dora was addressed.

Who wrote this memo? If it was somebody on the staff of the U.G.I.F., it suggests that Dora Bruder and her parents had been known to the U.G.I.F. for some time. Very likely Cécile Bruder, Dora's mother, in common with the majority of Jews living in extreme poverty with no other means of support, had turned to this organisation as a last resort. It was her only means of getting news of her husband, interned at Drancy since March, and of sending him food parcels. And she may have thought

101

that, with the help of the U.G.I.F., she would eventually find her daughter.

"Social workers attached to the police (Quai de Gesvres) will take the necessary action if required." In 1942, these consisted of twenty women attached to the Brigade for the Protection of Minors, a branch of the Criminal Investigation Department. They formed an autonomous section under a senior social worker.

I have found a photograph dating from this period. Two women aged about twenty-five. They are dressed in black – or navy-blue – uniform, with a sort of kepi sporting a badge of two intertwined Ps: Prefecture of Police. The woman on the left, a brunette with hair almost down to her shoulders, carries a satchel. The one on the right appears to be wearing lipstick. Behind the brunette, two wall-plaques read: POLICE SOCIAL SERVICES. Below this, an arrow, and underneath it: "Open 09.30h. to 12.00h." The writing on the lower plaque is half-obscured by the brunette's head and kepi. Nevertheless, one can read:

"DEPARTMENT OF . . .

INSPECTORS"

Underneath, an arrow: "Passage on Right. Door no. . . ."

We shall never know the number of this door.

What happened to Dora, I wonder, in the interval between 15 June, when she found herself in Clignancourt police station, and 17 June, the date of the "Memo to Mlle Salomon". Had she been allowed to leave the police station with her mother?

If she had been allowed to return to the Boulevard Ornano hotel with her mother – it was no distance, just down the Rue Hermel – it means that the social workers would have come for her three days later, after Mlle Salomon had made contact with the Quai des Gesvres.

But I have a feeling that things were not quite as straightforward as that. I have often taken the Rue Hermel, in both directions, to the Butte Montmartre and to the Boulevard Ornano, and try as I might, closing my eyes, I find it hard to picture Dora and her mother walking down this street on their way back to their hotel room on a sunny June afternoon as though it was just another day.

I believe that on 15 June, at Clignancourt police station, Dora and her mother were caught up in a chain reaction over which they no longer had control. Children are liable to expect more from life than their parents, and faced with adversity, their reaction is more violent. They go farther, much farther than their parents. And, thereafter, their parents are unable to protect them.

Confronted with the police, Mlle Salomon, social workers, German decrees and French laws, Cécile Bruder, with her yellow star, her husband interned in Drancy and her "state of penury", would have felt utterly defenceless. And quite unable to cope with Dora, a rebel who had more than once shown her determination to tear a hole in this net which had been thrown over her and her parents.

"In view of the fact that she has repeatedly run away, it seems advisable to have her admitted to a remand home for juveniles."

Perhaps Dora was taken from Clignancourt police station to the Dépôt at police headquarters, that being the usual practice. In which case, she would have known that huge, windowless basement, its cells, its straw mattresses heaped with Jewish women, prostitutes, "criminals" and "political" prisoners huddled together anyhow. She would have known the lice and the foul stink, and the wardresses, those terrifying black-clad nuns with little blue veils from whom it was useless to expect the least pity.

Or else she was taken directly to the Quai des Gesvres, open 09.30h. to 12.00h. She would have gone down the passage on the right, stopping outside the door the number of which I shall never know.

Either way, on 19 June 1942, she must have climbed into a police van, where she would have found five girls of her age already installed. Unless these five were picked up as the van did the rounds of police stations before taking them all to the internment centre of Tourelles, Boulevard Mortier, at the Porte des Lilas.

The Tourelles register for 1942 survives. On the cover is one word: WOMEN. It lists the names of internees in order of arrival. These women had been arrested for acts of resistance, for being Communist and, up to August 1942 in the case of Jews, for having failed to comply with German decrees: Jews were forbidden to go out after eight o'clock at night, compelled to wear the yellow star, forbidden to cross the demarcation line into the Free Zone, forbidden to use the telephone, to possess a bicycle, a radio . . .

The register has the following entry for 19 June 1942:

Arrivals 19 June 1942
439. 19.6.42. Bruder Dora. 25.2.26. Paris 12th.
French. 41 Bd Ornano. J. xx Drancy 13/8/42.

For the same date, there follow the names of five other girls, all about the same age as Dora:

440. 19.6.42. 5th Winerbett Claudine. 26.11.24. Paris 9th. French. 82 Rue des Moines. J. xx Drancy 13/8/42.

1. 19.6.42. 5th Stroblitz Zélie. 4.2.26. Paris 11th. French. 48 Rue Molière. Montreuil. J. Drancy 13/8/42.

2. 19.6.42. Isrealowicz Raca. 19.7.1924. Lodz. Ind. J. 26 Rue [illegible]. Deported by German authorities convoy 19.7.42.

3. 19.6.42 Nachmanowicz Marthe. 23.3.25. Paris. French. 258 Rue Marcadet. J. xx Drancy. 13/8/42.

4. 19.6.42, 5th Pitoun Yvonne. 27.1.25. Algiers. French. 3 Rue Marcel-Sembat. J. xx Drancy 13/8/42.

The police had allotted each girl a registration number. Dora's was 439. I don't know the meaning of 5th. The letter J stands for Jewish. In each case, Drancy 13/8/42 had been added on 13 August 1942; the day when the 300 Jewish women who were still interned at Tourelles were transferred to Drancy camp.

On that Thursday, 19 June, the day Dora arrived at Tourelles, the women were assembled on the barrack-square after breakfast. Three German officers were present. Jewish women between the ages of eighteen and forty were ordered to line up, backs turned. One of the Germans had ready a complete list of these women, and called out their names in the order written. The rest were returned to their rooms. The sixty-six women thus segregated from their companions were locked up in a large, empty room, without beds or chairs, where they remained in isolation for three days, a policeman guarding the door.

On Sunday 22 June, at five o'clock in the morning, buses arrived to take them to Drancy. That same day, they were deported in a convoy consisting of over 900 men. It was the first transport to leave France with women on board.

For the Jewish women in Tourelles, the hovering menace to which they had never quite been able to put a name and which, at times, they had succeeded in forgetting, had become fact. And in this oppressive atmosphere, Dora spent the first three days of her internment. On the Sunday morning, while it was still dark, she and her fellow internees watched through closed windows as the sixty-six women were driven away.

On 18 June, or else on the following morning, a desk clerk would have made out Dora's transfer warrant for Tourelles. Had this been done at Clignancourt police station, or at the Quai des Gesvres? The warrant had had to be filled out in duplicate and the copies handed, complete with ticks and signatures, to the guards on the police van. As he signed his name, did the clerk consider the implications of his act? After all, for him, it was merely a routine signature; and besides, the girl was being sent to a place still reassuringly designated by the Prefecture of Police as "Hostel. Supervised short-term accomodation."

*

I have managed to identify a few women among those who left Tourelles on Sunday 22 June at five o'clock in the morning and would have overlapped with Dora after her arrival on the Thursday.

Claude Bloch was thirty-two years old. She had been picked up on her way to Gestapo headquarters in the

Avenue Foch to ask for news of her husband, who had been arrested in December 1941. She was the only person on that transport to survive.

Josette Delimal was twenty-one. She and Claude Bloch met in the Dépôt at the Prefecture of Police and both were taken to Tourelles on the same day. According to Claude, "Josette had had a tough time before the war and hadn't built up the strength one draws from happy memories. She broke down completely. I did my best to comfort her. [. . .] When they took us to the dormitory to assign us to our beds, I refused to let them separate us. We were together until Auschwitz, where typhus soon carried her off." That is the extent of my knowledge about Josette Delimal. I only wish it were more.

Tamara Isserlis. She was twenty-four. A medical student. She was arrested at Cluny métro station "for concealing the French flag beneath the Star of David". Her identity card has been found and gives her address as 10 Rue de Buzenval, Saint-Cloud. She had an oval-shaped face, light-brown hair and dark eyes.

Ida Levine. Twenty-nine. A few of her letters to her family survive, written first from the Dépôt, then from Tourelles. She threw her last letter from the train at Bar-le-Duc station, where a railwayman posted it. She writes: "I'm writing this on a train to an unknown destination, but it's travelling east, so perhaps we're going quite far away . . ."

Hena: I shall call her by her forename. She was nineteen. She had got herself arrested because she and her boyfriend had burgled an apartment, stealing jewellery and cash to the value of 150,000 old francs. Perhaps, with this money, she dreamed of leaving France and escaping the threats hanging over her. She was taken before a magistrate and sentenced for theft. Being Jewish, instead of an ordinary prison, she was sent to Tourelles. I feel a certain solidarity with her act of burglary. In 1942, my father and his accomplices had plundered the S.K.F. warehouse on the Avenue de La Grande Armée of its stock of ball bearings, loading their loot on to lorries and transporting it back to the den on Avenue Hoche from which they operated their black market business. According to German decrees, Vichy laws and articles in the press, they were no better than vermin and common criminals, so they felt justified in behaving like outlaws in order to survive. For them, it was a point of honour. And I applaud them for it.

What I know about Hena amounts to almost nothing: she was born on 11 December 1922 at Pruszkow in Poland, and she lived at no. 42 Rue Oberkampf, the steeply sloping street I have so often climbed.

Annette Zelman. She was twenty-one years old. A blonde. She lived at no. 58 Boulevard de Strasbourg with a young man, Jean Jausion, the son of a professor of medicine. His first poems had been published in *Les Réverbères*, a Surrealist magazine which he had started with some friends just before the war.

Annette Zelman. Jean Jausion. In 1942, they were often to be seen together at the Café Flore. For a while they had hidden in the Free Zone. And then disaster struck. The story is summed up in a few words in a letter from a Gestapo officer:

21 May 1942 re. marriage between Jews and non-Jews.

It has come to my knowledge that the French national Jean Jausion (Aryan), aged 24, philosophy student, and the Jewess Anna Melka Zelman, born Nancy 6 October 1921, plan to marry over Whitsun.

The Jausion parents wish to prevent this union at all costs but lack the power to do so.

Consequently, I have taken the precaution of ordering the arrest of the Jewess Zelman and her internment in the camp at Tourelles barracks ...

And in a French police file:

Annette Zelman, Jewess, born Nancy 6 October 1921. French: arrested 23 May 1942. Confined in the Dépôt at the Prefecture of Police 23 May to 10 June, transferred to Germany 22 June. Reason for arrest: projected marriage to an Aryan, Jean Jausion. Couple signed a written statement renouncing all plans to marry at the express wish of Dr H. Jausion, who hoped that they would be dissuaded and the Zelman girl returned to her family with nothing to fear.

But this doctor with his strange methods of dissuasion was too trusting: the police failed to return Annette Zelman to her family.

In 1944, Jean Jausion went off to be a war correspondent. In a copy of a newspaper dated 11 November 1944, I came across the following announcement:

Missing. The management of our sister paper *Le Franc-Tireur** would be grateful to anybody having information about the disappearance of one of its contributors, Jean Jausion, born Toulouse 20 August 1917, domiciled Paris, 21 Rue Théodore-de-Banville. Left 6 September on an assignment for *Franc-Tireur*, accompanied by a young couple named Lecomte, former maquisards,† in a black Citroen 11, front-wheel drive, registration RN 6283, bearing a white *Franc-Tireur* sticker at the rear.

---

* An underground Resistance newspaper which was published openly after the Liberation of Paris in August 1944.
† Members of the anti-German paramilitary resistance movement in France during World War II.

I heard that Jean Jausion launched his car at a German infantry column. He fired a machine gun at them before they had a chance to shoot and give him the death which he sought.

A book by Jean Jausion came out the following year, in 1945. It was entitled *Un Homme marche dans la ville*.

Two years ago, on one of the bookstalls along the Seine, I happened to find the last letter written by a man who was on the transport of 22 June with Claude Bloch, Josette Delimal, Tamara Isserlis, Hena, Jean Jausion's girl-friend Annette . . .

The fact that the letter was for sale, like any other manuscript, suggests that the sender and his family had disappeared in their turn. A square of thin paper covered back and front in minuscule handwriting, it was written from Drancy camp by a certain Robert Tartakovsky. I have discovered that he was born in Odessa on 24 November 1902, and that, before the war, he wrote a column on art for *L'Illustration*. Today, fifty years later, on Wednesday, 29 January 1997, I reproduce his letter.

Yesterday, I was picked to go. I've been mentally prepared for a long time. The camp is panic-stricken, many men are crying, they are afraid. The only thing bothering me is that most of the clothes I keep asking for have still not arrived. I have sent off a voucher for a clothes parcel: shall I get what I need in time? I don't want my mother or any of you to worry. I'll do my utmost to keep safe and well. If you don't hear from me, be patient, if necessary go to the Red Cross. Ask the Saint-Lambert police (Town Hall XVe), Vaugirard métro, to return the documents seized on 3/5. Be sure and ask about my certificate of volunteers enlistment, Regimental no. 10107, it may be at the camp and I don't know if they'll let me have it back. Please take a cast of Albertine to Mme BIANOVICI, 14 Rue Deguerry, Paris XIe, it's for a friend in my hut. She'll give you 1200 francs for it. Write first to be sure of finding her in. I approached M. Gompel, an internee at Drancy, and the sculptor is to be invited to exhibit at Les Trois Quartiers. Should the gallery want the entire edition, keep back three casts, saying either that they've been sold or else reserved for the publisher. If you think the mould will bear it, you can make two extra casts *following the said request.* Don't distress yourselves too much. I wish Marthe to go on holiday. Never imagine that no news is bad news. If you get this note in time, send the maximum number of food parcels, that way, the weight will be less carefully checked. Anything glass will be sent back, and knives, forks, razor blades, pens etc. are forbidden. Even needles. But I'll manage somehow. Army biscuits or unleavened bread welcome. In one of my regular letter-cards I mention a friend PERSIMAGI see Swedish embassy on his behalf (Irène), he's even taller than me and his clothes are in tatters (see Gattégno, 13 Rue Grande-Chaumière). A bar or two of good soap, some shaving soap, a shaving brush, tooth-brush, nailbrush, all welcome, I'm trying to think of everything at once, to mix the practical with all the other things I have to say to you. Nearly a thousand of us are to go. There are also Aryans in the camp. They are forced to wear the Jewish insignia. Yesterday, SS Captain Doncker arrived at the camp, scattering people in all directions. Advise our friends to get away somewhere if they can, for here one must abandon all hope. We may be sent to Compiègne before we leave for good, I'm not sure. I shan't be sending back any laundry, I'll do it here. The cowardice of most people here appals me. What effect will it have once we're there, I wonder. If you can, go and see Mme de Salzmann, not to ask her for anything in particular, just for information. Perhaps I'll get a chance to meet the person whom Jacqueline wanted to get released. Urge my mother to be very careful, people are being arrested daily, some here are very young, 17, 18, others as old as 72. Till Monday morning, you can send me parcels as often as you like. It's not true that they no longer accept parcels at the usual addresses, don't take no for an answer, telephone the U.G.I.F. at the Rue de la Bienfaisance. I didn't mean to alarm you in my previous letters, was only surprised not to have received the clothes I'll need for the journey. I'll be sending my watch back for Marthe, probably also my pen, I'll entrust them to B. Put nothing perishable in food parcels in case things have to be forwarded to me. Photographs without letters in food parcels or underwear. I'll probably send back the art books for which my warmest thanks. Doubtless I'll be spending the winter there, don't worry, I'm prepared. Re-read my cards. You'll see which things I've been asking for from the first and have slipped my mind. Darning wool. Scarf.

Sterogyl 15. My mother's metal box, as sugar crumbles. What upsets me is that all deportees have their heads shaved, it makes you even more conspicuous than the insignia. In the event of dispersal, I'll go on sending news via the Salvation Army, warn Irène.

Saturday 20 June 1942 – My dear ones, the case arrived yesterday, thank you for everything. I'm not sure, but I fear our departure is put forward. I am to have my head shaved today. From tonight, deportees will probably be confined to a special hut and closely guarded, even to the lavatory and back. A sinister atmosphere hovers over the camp. I doubt that we'll be going via Compiègne. I know we are to be given three days' rations for the journey. I'm afraid I'll be gone before more parcels arrive, but don't worry, the last one was very generous and since being here I've put aside all chocolate and jams, and the large sausage. Keep calm, I'll be thinking of you. I wanted to give Marthe a recording of *Petruchska* on 28/7, the complete set of 4. Saw B. last night to thank him for all he has done, he knows that I've been defending Leroy's sculptures to key people here. Am delighted with latest photos but haven't shown them to B., I apologized for not giving him one but said he could always ask you. Sad to interrupt the edition, but there'll be time if I'm back soon enough. I like Leroy's work, would gladly have published a reduction within my means, can't stop thinking about it, even though we are to leave in a few hours.

Please do all you can for my mother, by which I don't mean that you should neglect your personal affairs. Tell Irène that as my mother's neighbour I wish her to do likewise. Try to telephone Dr André ABADI (if still in Paris). Tell him I met the person whose address he knows on 1 May and was arrested on 3 May (was this mere coincidence?). This incoherent letter probably surprises you; but the atmosphere is hard to bear, it's 6.30 a.m. I'm about to send back everything I'm not taking with me, I'm afraid of taking too much. The searchers are liable to throw out a case at the last moment if there's no room, it depends on their mood (they're from the Jewish Affairs police, either pamperers or pillagers). Still, that has its uses. I'll get my belongings sorted out. Don't panic the moment you stop hearing from me, keep calm, wait patiently and with trust, have faith in me, reassure my mother that, having seen departures for the Beyond (as I told you) I prefer to be on this journey. My main regret is to be parted from my pen, not to be allowed paper (an absurd thought crosses my mind: knives are forbidden, and I don't even possess a simple key to open a tin of sardines). I'm not putting on a brave face, don't have the heart in this atmosphere: a lot of the sick and infirm are also picked for deportation. I'm also thinking of Rd, hoping that he is safe at last. I left all sorts of things with Jacques Daumal. Probably no point in moving my books out of the house now, I leave it to you. Let's hope we have good weather for the journey! Make sure my mother receives all her allowances, get the U.G.I.F. to help her. I hope you've made it up with Jacqueline by now, she is a strange girl, but good at heart (the sky is clearing, it's going to be a fine day). I don't know if you got my usual card, or if I'll get your answer before we leave. I think of my mother, of you. Of all my loving friends who did so much to help me keep my freedom. Heartfelt thanks to those who helped me "get through" the winter. I'm leaving this letter unfinished, it's time to pack my bag. Back soon. A note in case I can't finish, pen and watch to Marthe whatever my mother says. I kiss you goodbye dearest Maman, and you my dear ones, with all my love. Be brave. It's 7 a.m., back soon.

Twice in April 1966 I spent a Sunday in the eastern districts of Paris, searching for traces of Dora Bruder in the areas around the Holy Heart of Mary and Tourelles. I felt this was best done on a Sunday when the town is deserted, at the lowest ebb of the tide.

Nothing is left of the Holy Heart of Mary. A modern apartment block stands at the corner of the Rue de la Gare-de-Reuilly and the Rue de Picpus. The section occupying the former site of the convent's tree-shaded wall now displays the last odd numbers of the Rue de la Gare-de-Reuilly. Opposite and a little further along on the even-numbered side, the street remains unchanged.

It is hard to believe that, one July morning in 1942, while Dora was interned at Tourelles, the police had come to arrest nine children and adolescents at no. 48*bis*, where the windows once overlooked the garden of the Holy Heart of Mary. It is a five-storey building in light-coloured brick. On each floor, two windows flank two smaller windows. No. 40 next door is a greyish building, recessed and fronted by an iron gate set in a low brick wall. The small houses opposite, on the stretch of pavement that once bordered the convent wall, have remained as they were. No. 54, just before you reach the Rue de Picpus, used to be a café owned by a Mlle Lenzi.

All of a sudden, I felt certain that, on the night when she made her escape, Dora had slipped away from the convent by the Rue de la Gare-de-Reuilly. I could visualise her hugging the convent wall. Perhaps streets named after a station evoke thoughts of escape.

I wandered around the neighbourhoods, weighed down after a while by the sadness of those other Sundays when it was time to return to the convent. I felt sure that she had left the métro at Nation. She would have put off the moment when she must enter the gate and cross the courtyard. She prolonged her walk, choosing streets at random. It grew dark. The Avenue de Saint-Mandé is quiet, bordered by trees. I forget whether or not there is a stretch of open ground. Some way along is the entrance to the old Picpus métro station. Did she ever emerge from there? In comparison with the Avenue de Saint-Mandé, the Avenue Picpus, on the right, is cold and desolate. Treeless, as I remember. Ah, the loneliness of returning on those Sunday evenings.

The Boulevard Mortier slopes downhill, to the south. On my way there, that Sunday of 28 April 1996, I took the following route: Rue des Archives, Rue de Bretagne, Rue des-Filles-du-Calvaire. Then the uphill slope of the Rue Oberkampf, where Hena had lived.

To the right, the Rue des Pyrénées, offering a vista of trees. The Rue de Ménilmontant, the apartment block at no. 140 deserted in the glare of the sun. For the last part of the Rue Saint-Fargeau, I seemed to be traversing an abandoned village.

Plane trees line the Boulevard Mortier, and still there, at the top, just before you reach the Porte des Lilas, are the old Tourelles barracks

On that particular Sunday, the boulevard was empty, lost in a silence so deep that I could hear the rustling of the planes. The buildings of the former barracks are hidden behind a high perimeter wall. I followed it. Affixed to it, there was a sign that read:

MILITARY ZONE

FILMING OR PHOTOGRAPHY PROHIBITED

I told myself that nobody remembers anything any more. A no-man's-land lay beyond that wall, a zone of emptiness and oblivion. Unlike the convent in the Rue de Picpus, the twin blocks of Tourelles barracks had not been pulled down, but they might as well have been.

And yet, from time to time, beneath this thick layer of amnesia, one can certainly sense something, an echo, distant, muted, but of what, precisely, it is impossible to say. Like finding oneself on the edge of a magnetic field and having no pendulum with which to pick up its radiations. The sign had been put up out of suspicion and a guilty conscience: "Military zone. Filming or photography prohibited".

In another part of Paris, when I was twenty, I remember having the same sensation of emptiness as I had had when confronted by the Tourelles wall, and without really knowing the reason why.

I had a girlfriend who lived in various borrowed flats and country houses. I would regularly take advantage of this to relieve their libraries of art books and numbered editions, which I then sold. One day, when we were by ourselves in a flat on the Rue du Regard, I stole an antique music box, and also, after rifling the wardrobes, several very smart suits, a few shirts and about ten pairs of handmade shoes. Searching the trade directory for a second-hand dealer to whom I could re-sell these items, I found one in the Rue des Jardins-Saint-Paul.

This street runs at right angles to the Quai des Célestins and the Seine and intersects the Rue de Charlemagne near the school where, the year before, I had gone through the ordeal of my *baccalauréat*. One of the last buildings on the right, just before the Rue de Charlemagne, had a rusting iron curtain at street level, half raised. I pushed my way into a junk shop piled high with furniture, clothes, ironwork, automobile spares. The middle-aged man who greeted me was most obliging, offering to come and collect the "goods" in a few days' time.

Having taken my leave of him, I walked down the Rue des Jardins-Saint-Paul towards the Seine. All the buildings on the left-hand side of the street had recently been demolished as had the other buildings behind them. In their place, nothing but a wasteland, itself surrounded by half-demolished walls. On these walls, open to the sky, one could still make out the patterned paper of what was once a bedroom, the outline of a chimney breast. One might have thought that the area had just been bombed, and the view of the Seine at the bottom of the street only increased the impression of emptiness.

*

On the following Sunday, by appointment, the second-hand dealer came to my girlfriend's father's place on the Boulevard Kellermann near the Porte de Gentillly where I was to hand over the "goods". He loaded the music box, suits, shirts and shoes on to his van, giving me 700 old francs for the lot.

He suggested going for a drink. We stopped at one of two cafés opposite Charlety stadium.

He inquired what I did for a living. I didn't quite know what to say. In the end, I told him that I had dropped out of school, I questioned him in my turn. The junk shop in the Rue de Jardins-Saint-Paul belonged to his cousin, who was also his business partner. He himself had another shop, near the flea market at the Porte de Clignancourt. It turned out that he came from a local family of Polish Jews.

I was the one who brought up the subject of the war and the Occupation. He had been eighteen at the time. He remembered that, one Saturday, the police had made a swoop to arrest Jews in the Porte de Saint-Ouen flea markets, and that he had escaped this round-up by a miracle. What had shocked him most was that one of the police inspectors had been a woman.

I mentioned the wasteland stretching to the foot of the apartment buildings on Boulevard Ney, and which I had noticed on the Saturdays when my mother took me to the flea markets. It was there that he had lived with his family. Rue Élisabeth-Rolland. He was amazed that I should make a note of its name. The district was known as the Plain. Completely demolished after the war, it was now a sports field.

Talking to him, I thought of my father, whom I hadn't seen for a long time. When he was nineteen, my age, before he had lost himself in dreams of high finance, my father had lived by wheeling and dealing at the gates of Paris: he smuggled cans of petrol for re-sale to garage owners, spirits and various other goods. All without paying excise duty.

As we parted, the dealer said amiably that if I had any more items for him, I could reach him at the Rue des Jardins-Saint-Paul. And he gave me an extra hundred francs, no doubt touched by my air of being a guileless, likeable young chap.

I've forgotten his face. I remember nothing about him apart from his name. He could easily have met Dora Bruder around the Porte de Clignancourt, around the Plain. They were the same age and lived in the same neighbourhood. Perhaps he knew the full story of the times she spent on the run . . . There are flukes, encounters, coincidences like that, and we shall never take advantage of them . . . I was thinking of that, this autumn, when I went back to explore the area around the Rue des Jardins-Saint-Paul. The junk shop with its iron curtain was no more, and the surrounding buildings had been restored. Once again, I had a sense of emptiness. And I understood why. After the war, most buildings in the district had been pulled down, methodically, in accordance with a government plan. To the extent that, due for demolition, this zone had been allotted a name and number: Block 16. I have found photographs. One shows the Rue des Jardins-Saint-Paul with the houses on the left-hand side still standing. Another, the half-demolished buildings beside Saint-Gervais church and around the Hôtel de Sens. Another, a wasteland along the banks of the Seine, with pedestrians crossing between two redundant pavements: all that remains of the Rue des Nonnains-d'Hyères. And on this wasteland, they have built row upon row of houses, altering the course of an old street in the process.

The façades are rectangular, the windows square, the cement the colour of amnesia. The street lamps throw out a cold light. Here and there, a decorative touch, some artificial flowers: a bench, a square, some trees. They have not been content with putting up a sign, like that on the wall of Tourelles barracks: "Filming or photography prohibited." They have obliterated everything in order to build a sort of Swiss village, in order that nobody, ever again, would question its neutrality.

The patches of wallpaper which I had seen thirty years before in the Rue des Jardins-Saint-Paul were remnants of former bedsits – rooms which had been home to young people of Dora's age until the day when the police had come for them in July 1942. The list of their names is always associated with the same streets. And the street-names and house-numbers no longer correspond to anything.

When I was seventeen, Tourelles had meant no more than a name I had read at the back of a book by Jean Genet, *Miracle de la Rose*. There he lists the places where the book was written: LA SANTÉ, TOURELLES PRISON, 1943. Shortly after Dora Bruder's departure from Tourelles, he too had been imprisoned there as a common criminal, and their paths may have crossed. *Miracle de la Rose* is not only impregnated with memories of the penal settlement at Mettray – one of those remand homes where they had wanted to send Dora – but also, I now realise, of La Santé and Tourelles.

I know sentences from this book by heart. I remember one in particular: "What that child taught me is that the true roots of Parisian slang lie in its sad tenderness." This phrase evokes Dora Bruder for me so well that I feel I knew her. The children with Polish or Russian or

Romanian names who were forced to wear the yellow star were so Parisian that they merged effortlessly into the façades, the apartment blocks, the pavements, the infinite shades of grey which belong to Paris alone. Like Dora Bruder, they all spoke with the Parisian accent, using a slang whose sad tenderness Jean Genet had recognized.

*

At Tourelles, when Dora was a prisoner there, one could receive parcels, and also visits, on Thursdays and Sundays. And, on Tuesdays, one could attend Mass. The guards held roll-call at eight o'clock in the morning. The detainees stood to attention at the end of their beds. At lunch in the refectory there was nothing but cabbage. Exercise-period on the barrack-square. Supper at six o'clock. Another roll-call. Once a fortnight, a trip to the shower, two at a time, accompanied by a guard. Whistle blasts. You waited. To receive a visit, you had to write a letter to the prison director, and you never knew if he would give his authorization.

Visits took place after lunch, in the refectory. Those who came had their bags searched by the guards. Parcels were opened. Often, for no reason, visits were cancelled, and the detainees informed only an hour beforehand.

Among the women whom Dora could have met at Tourelles were some who were known to the Germans as "Jews' friends": there are about ten of them, "Aryan"

Frenchwomen who, in June, from the first day that Jews had been obliged to wear the yellow star, had had the courage to wear it themselves as a sign of solidarity, but in imaginative ways that ridiculed the occupying authorities. One had fixed the yellow star to the collar of her dog. Another had embroidered hers with PAPOU.* Another, with JENNY. Another had attached eight stars to her belt, each bearing a letter, spelling out the word VICTOIRE. All had been arrested in the street and taken to the nearest police station. Then to the Dépôt at the Prefecture of Police. Then to Tourelles. Then, on 13 August, to Drancy camp. Between them, these so-called "Jews' friends" had the following occupations: Typist. Newsagent. Paperseller. Cleaner. Post Office worker. Student.

*

In August, the number of arrests multiplied. Women no longer even passed through the Dépôt, but were taken directly to Tourelles. Dormitories meant for twenty now held double that number. With overcrowding, it was suffocatingly hot. Anxiety mounted. It was common knowledge that Tourelles was merely a marshalling yard where, from one day to the next, one might be shunted off to an unknown destination.

Two groups of Jewish women, about a hundred in all, had already left for Drancy camp on 19 and 27 July. Among

* A native of Papua New Guinea.

them, an eighteen-year-old Pole, Raca Isrealowicz, who had arrived at Tourelles on the same day as Dora, probably in the same police van. And who was doubtless one of her neighbours in the dormitory.

On the evening of 12 August, a rumour spread through Tourelles that all Jewish Women and "Jews' friends" were to leave for Drancy camp on the following day.

At ten o'clock on the morning of 13 August, the interminable roll-call began under the chestnut trees on the barrack square. A last meal. A meagre ration which left you famished.

The buses arrived. In sufficent numbers – apparently – for each prisoner to have a seat. Dora included. It was a Thursday, visiting day.

The convoy formed up. It was escorted by helmeted policemen on motorcycles. It took the same route which one takes for Roissy airport today. Over fifty years have passed. By building a motorway, razing houses to the ground and thus transforming the landscape of this north-eastern suburb, they have rendered it, like the former Block 16, as neutral and grey as possible. But the blue road-signs on the road to the airport still bear the old names: DRANCY or ROMAINVILLE. And, stranded and forgotten on the verge of the motorway, near the Porte de Bagnolet, there is an old wooden barn on which someone has painted this name, clearly legible: DUREMORD.*

* This evokes the French term for guilt: "*Du remord*".

*

At Drancy, among the milling crowds, Dora found her
father. He had been interned there since March. That
particular August, as at the Dépôt at the Prefecture of
Police, as at Tourelles, the camp filled up day by day with
an increasing flood of men and women. Some came in
their thousands by goods trains from the Free Zone.
Many hundreds of women, forcibly separated from their
children, came from the camps at Beaune-la-Rolande
and Pithiviers. And, from 15 August onwards, after their
mothers had been deported, the children arrived in their
turn, 4,000 of them. In many cases, their names, hastily
scribbled on their clothes before they left Pithiviers and
Beaune-la-Rolande, were no longer legible. Unidentified
child no. 122. Unidentified child no. 146. Girl aged three.
First name Monique. Unidentified.

*

Because of the overcrowding in the camp, and in antici-
pation of the convoys still to arrive from the Free Zone,
on 2 and 5 September the authorities decided to transfer
Jews with French nationality from Drancy to Pithiviers.
Four girls who had arrived at Tourelles on the same day
as Dora, Claudine Winerbett, Zélie Strohlitz, Marthe
Nachmanowiccz, Yvonne Pitoun, all aged sixteen or
seventeen, left on this convoy of some 1,500 French

Jews. They were probably under the illusion that their nationality would protect them. Dora, being French, could have left with them. The reason she didn't do so is easy to guess: she preferred to stay with her father.

Father and daughter left Drancy on 18 September, in company with thousands of other men and women, on a convoy of trains bound for Auschwitz.

*

Dora's mother, Cécile Bruder, was arrested on 16 July 1942, the day of the great round-up, and interned at Drancy. She was re-united with her husband for a few days while their daughter was at Tourelles. Doubtless because she was born in Budapest and the authorities had not yet received orders to deport Hungarian Jews, Cécile Bruder was released from Drancy on 25 July.

Had she been able to visit Dora at Tourelles, one Thursday or Sunday, during that summer of 1942? On 9 January 1943, she was once again interned in Drancy camp and, on 11 February 1943, five months after her husband and daughter, she was put on a convoy for Auschwitz.

*

On Saturday 19 September, the day after Dora and her father left, the occupying authorities imposed a curfew in retaliation for a bomb placed in the Cinéma Rex. Nobody was allowed out from three o'clock that afternoon till the following morning. The city was deserted, as if to mark Dora's absence.

Ever since, the Paris wherein I have tried to retrace her steps has remained as silent and deserted as it was on that day. I walk through empty streets. For me, they are always empty, even at dusk, during the rush-hour, when the crowds are hurrying towards the mouths of the métro. I think of her in spite of myself, sensing an echo of her presence in this neighbourhood or that. The other evening, it was near the Gare du Nord.

I shall never know how she spent her days, where she hid, in whose company she passed the winter months of her first escape, or the few weeks of spring when she escaped for the second time. That is her secret. A poor and precious secret which not even the executioners, the decrees, the occupying authorities, the Dépôt, the barracks, the camps, history, time – everything that corrupts and destroys you – have been able to take away from her.